ART

FOR YOUR IMAGINATION

Book Three:

Copyright © 2021 Beverley Kornelsen

All rights reserved. No part of this book may be stored, reproduced, distributed, or transmitted in any manner whatsoever without the prior written permission of the publisher.

Contact: BevKornel@gmail.com

Printed by Amazon

ISBN-13: 979-87057-469-5-8

Previous books in this series:

ART FOR YOUR IMAGINATION
(Contains Images 1 – 41)

ART FOR YOUR IMAGINATION BOOK TWO
(Contains Images 42 – 102)

This third volume begins with Image 103

WHAT DO YOU SEE?

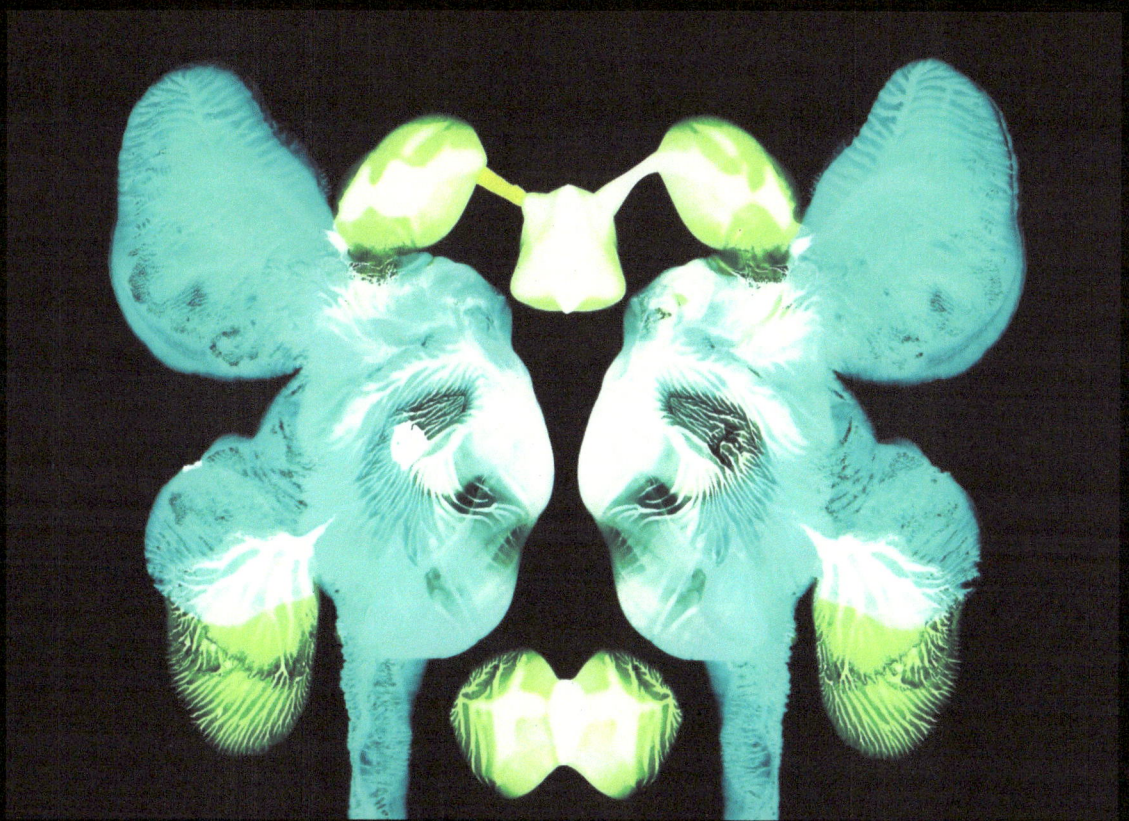

Image 103

Welcome to the third book in the *ART FOR YOUR IMAGINATION* series. Like the other volumes, you'll get the most enjoyment if you don't rush but give your imagination lots of time to process what your eyes are seeing. Look at the whole, and at the smaller details; look close up and farther away. The more you look, the more you will see.

In addition to never before seen images, some of the shapes in this book may have appeared in one of the first two volumes. They have been re-imagined as negatives of the originals, so have different colours featured on a new black background.

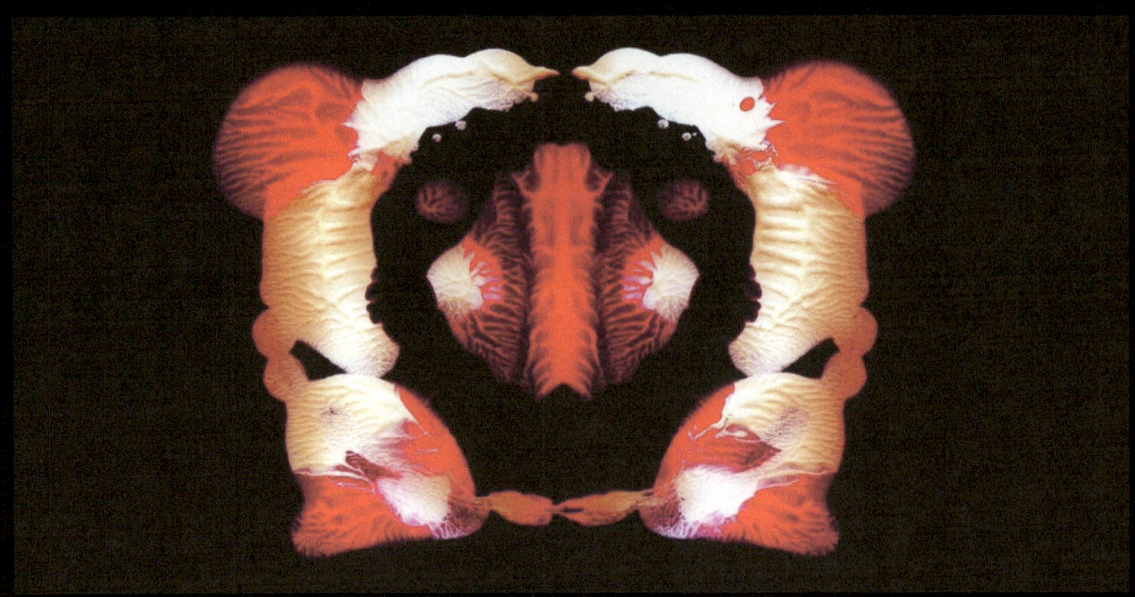

Image 104

    All the images were created with a vertical line of symmetry which results in not only a pleasing balance, but when combined with their organic forms, explains why most people see resemblances to living things—cute living things I might add. If you happen to see a lot of scary or disturbing scenes, you probably should consult a psychologist!

    In the red and white image above, I see two different animals depending on whether I focus on the inside negative or outside colour. On the inside, I see a black duck head with red eyes and a red and white bill. If I include everything, I see a bear with red ears, white hair parted on the top, and a black face with red eyes, a narrow nose and white cheeks. What do you see?

    If you feel like sharing, you can have some fun by asking your friends and family to describe what they see.

    If you want a quiet distraction, it can be meditative to pick an image and simply focus on its colourations.

    However you decide to use this book, I hope it helps you to relax. Enjoy!

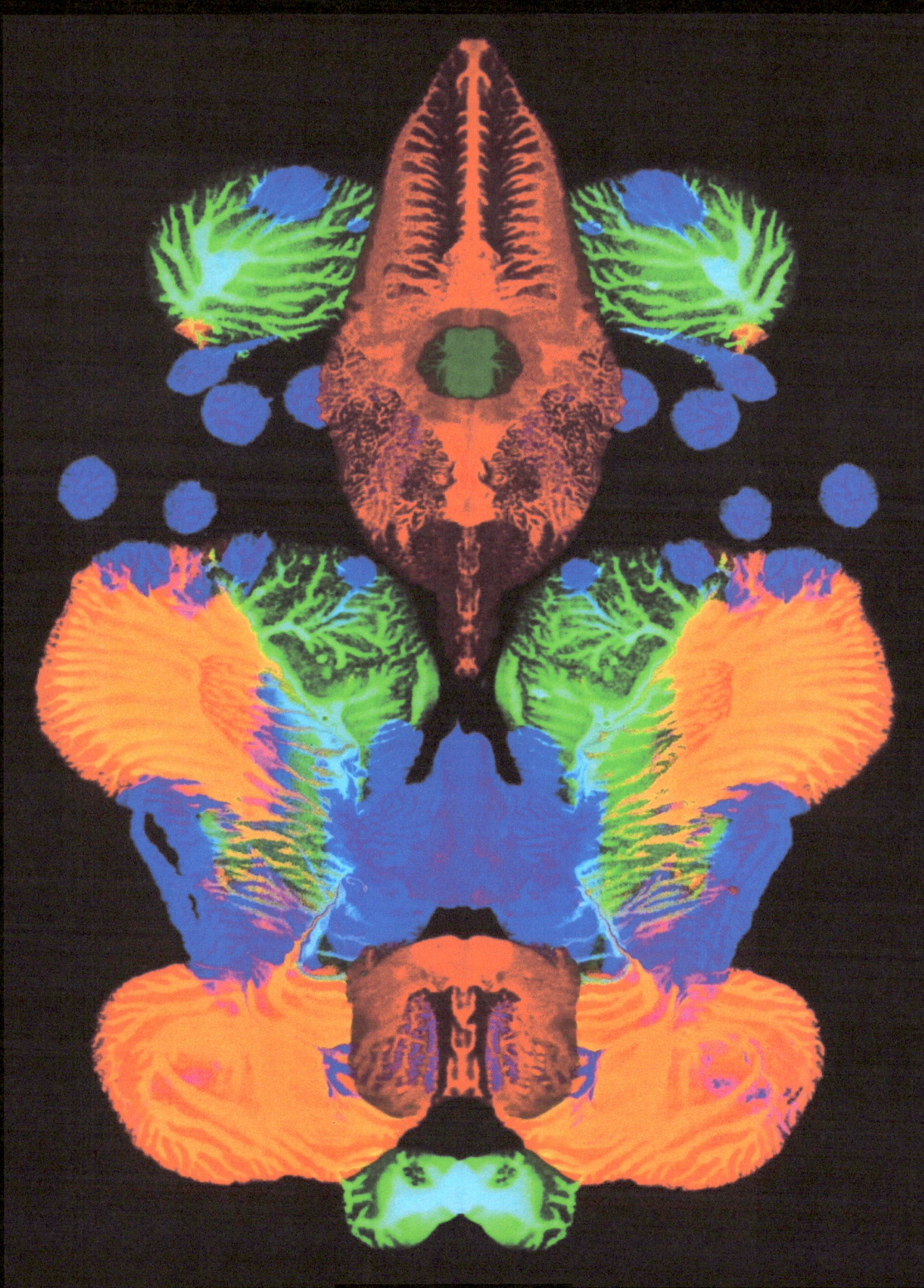

Image 105

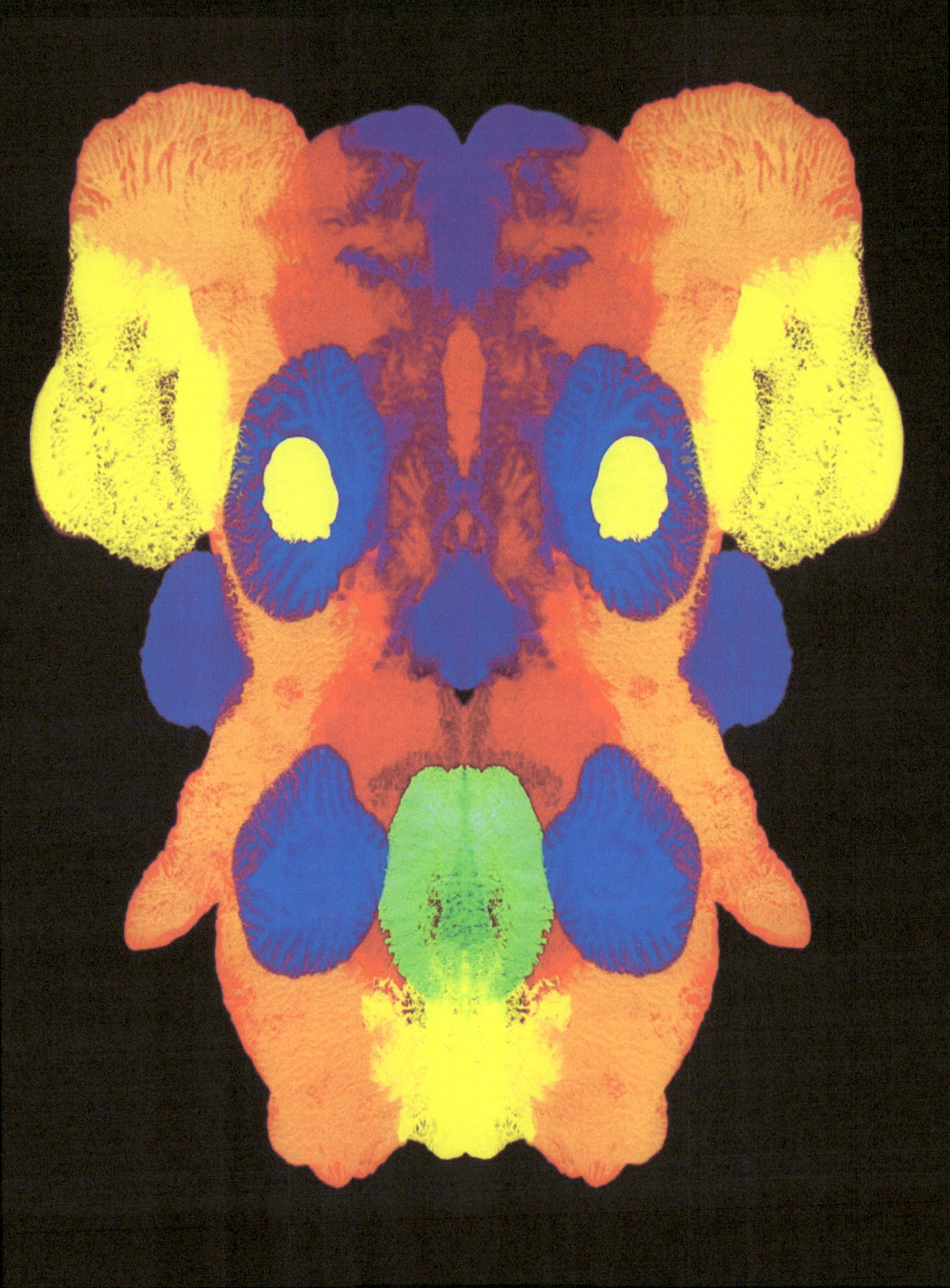

Image 106

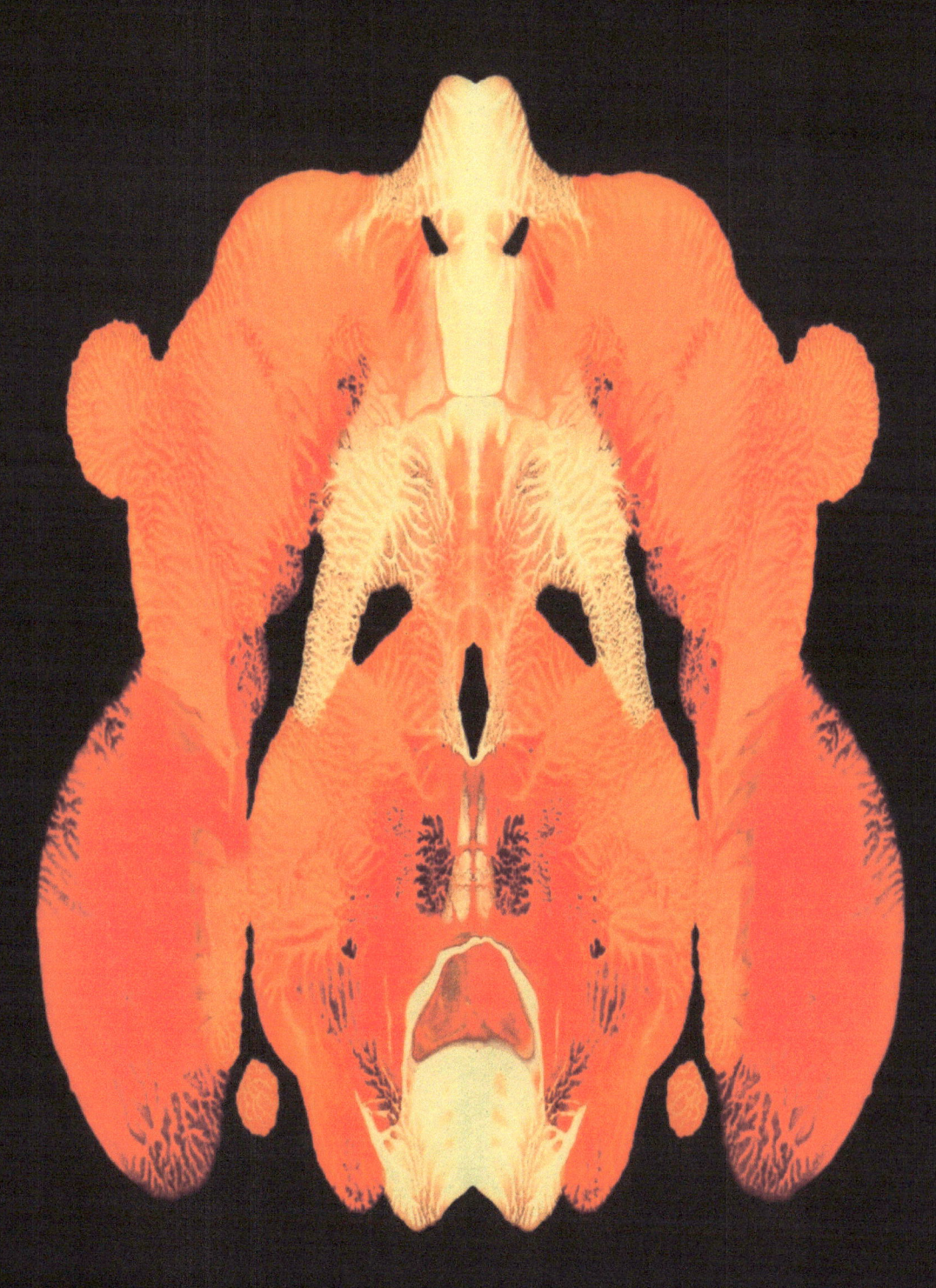

Image 107

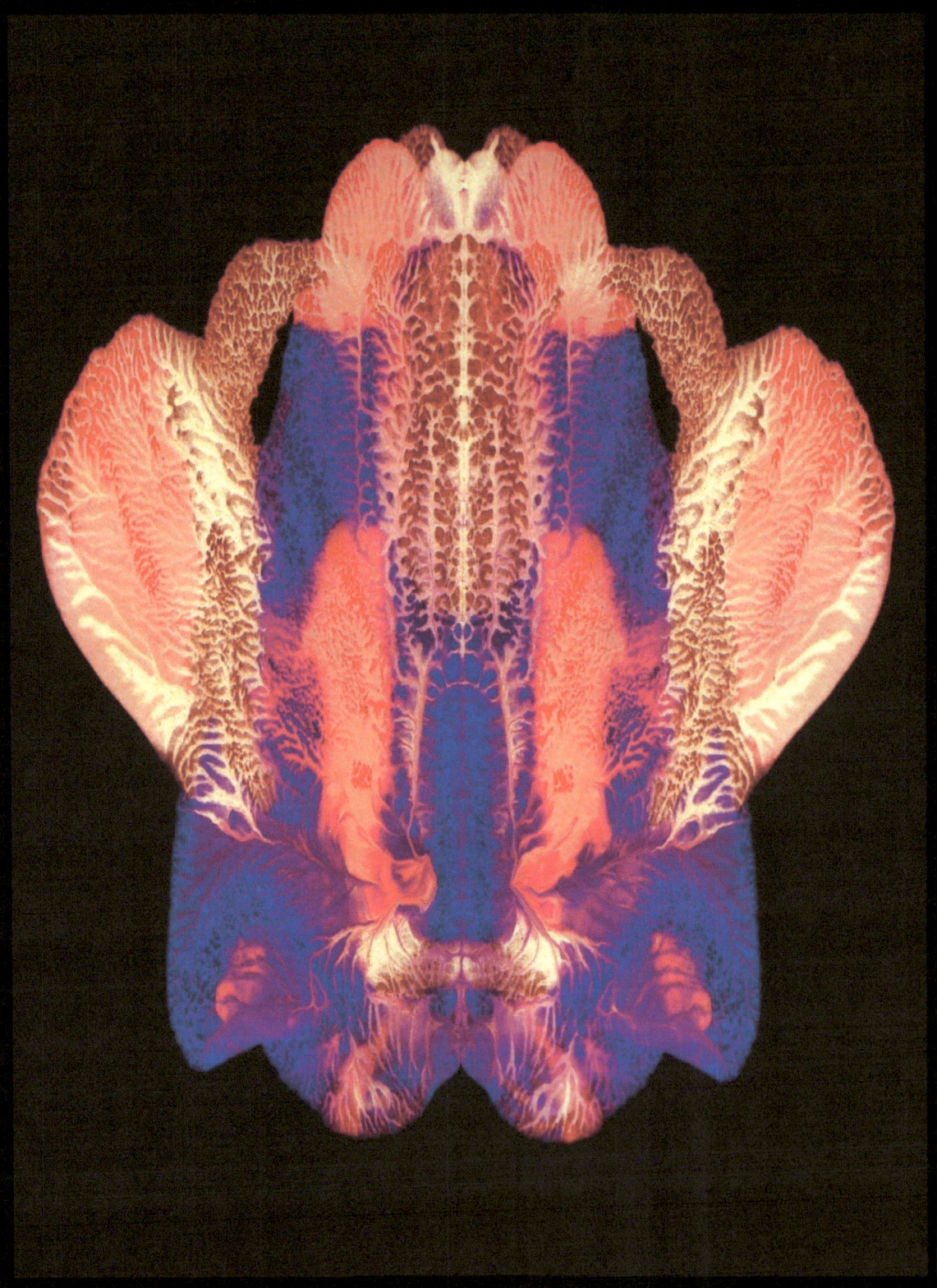

Image 108

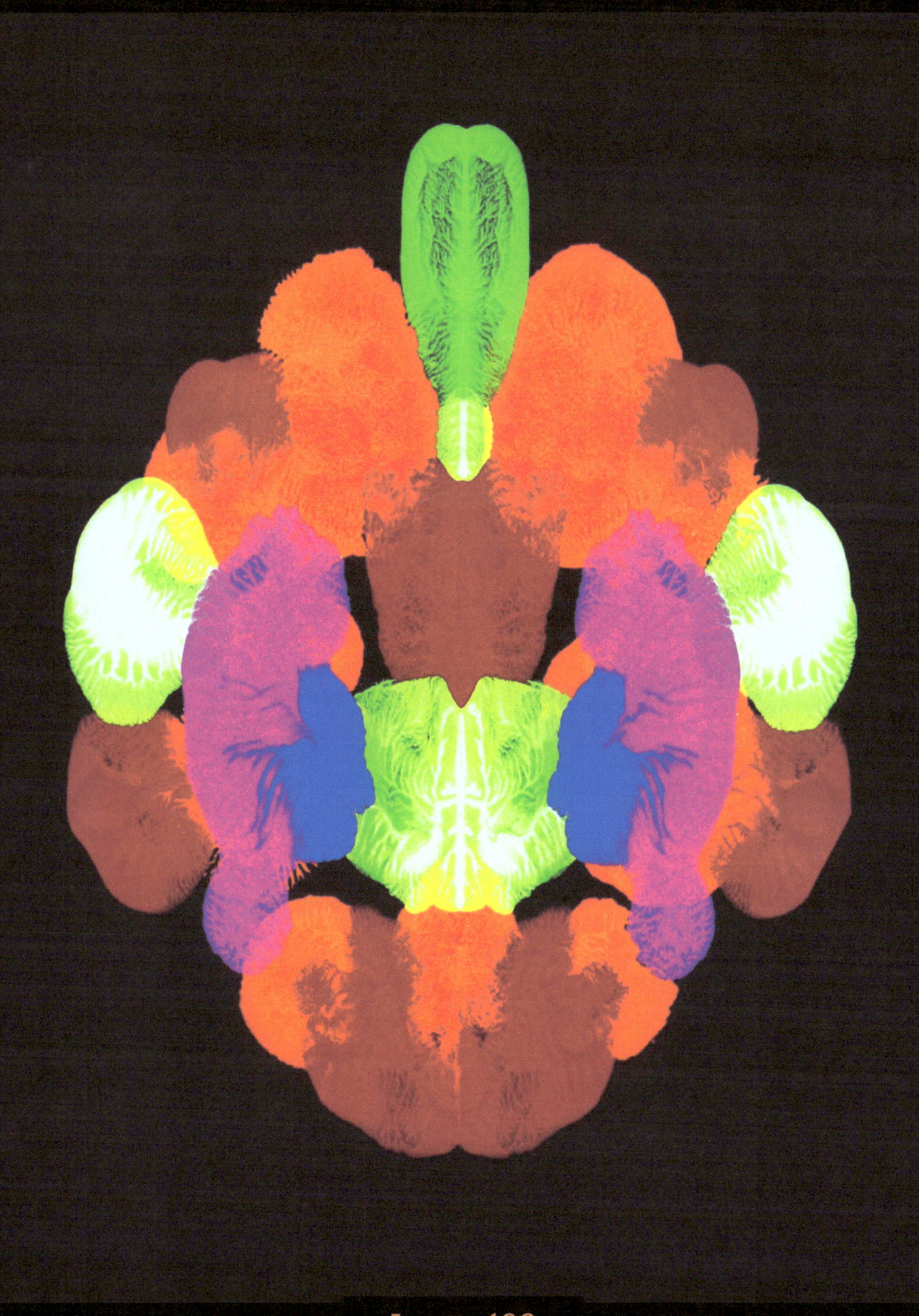
Image 109

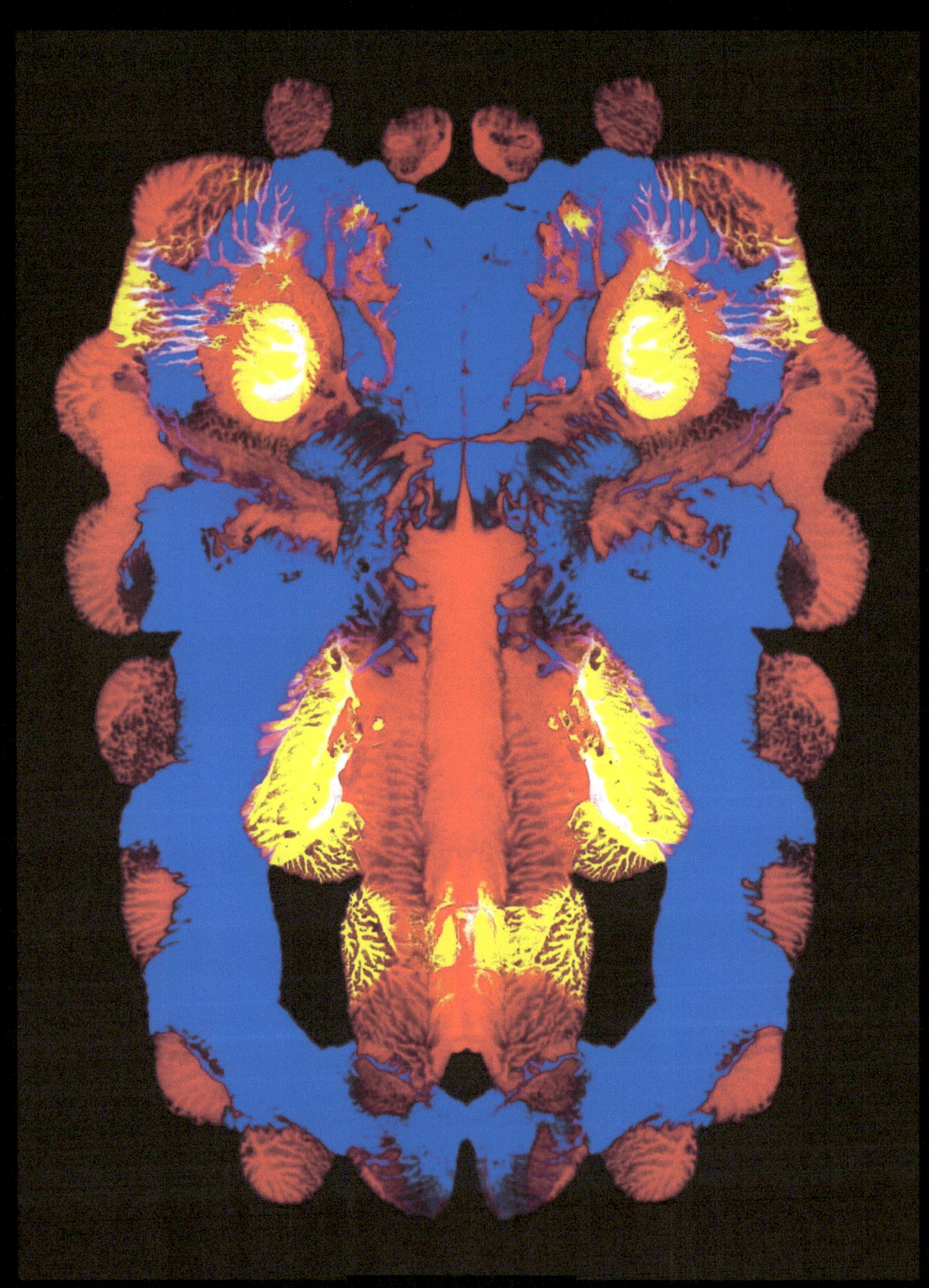

Image 110

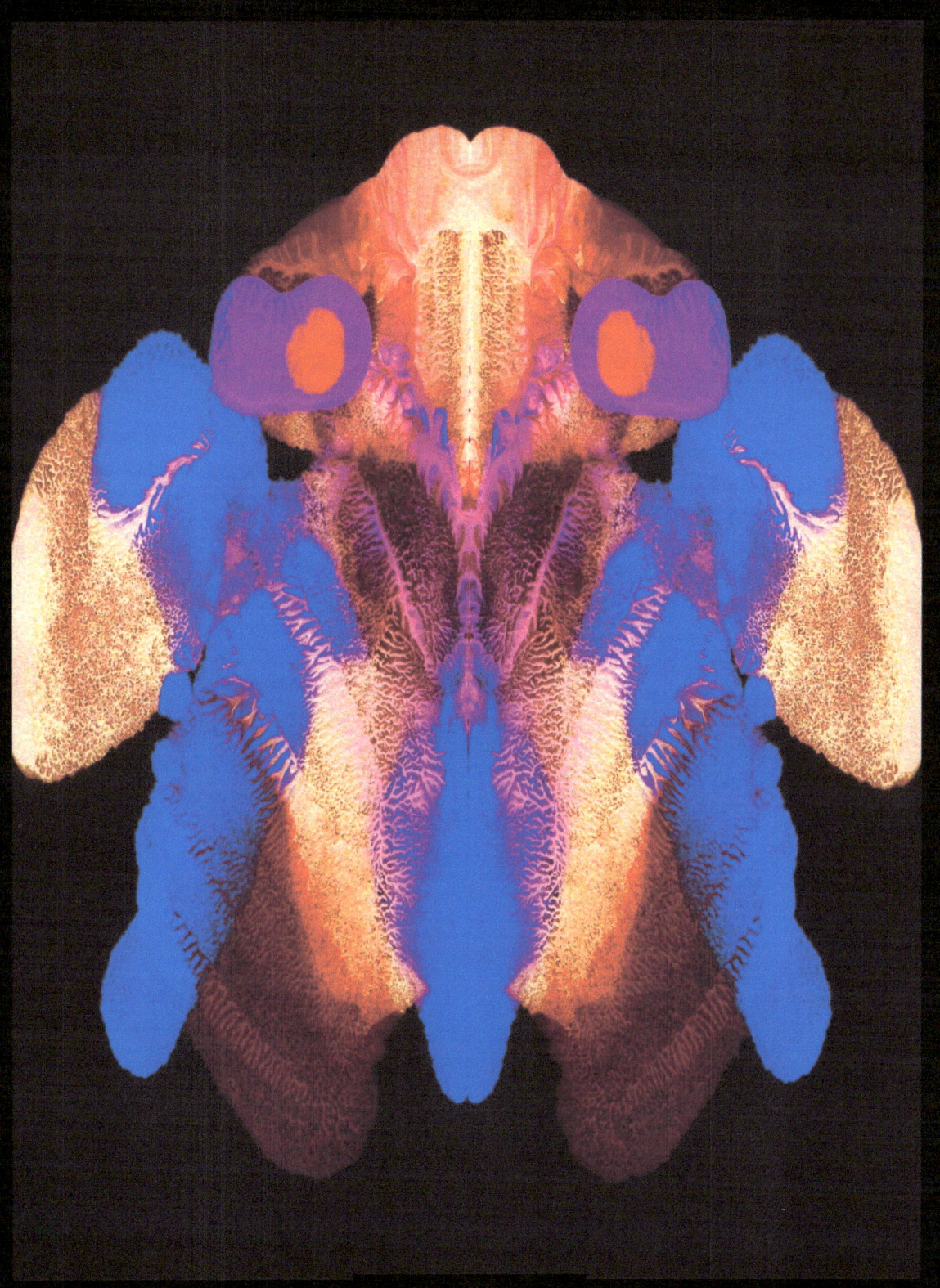

Image 111

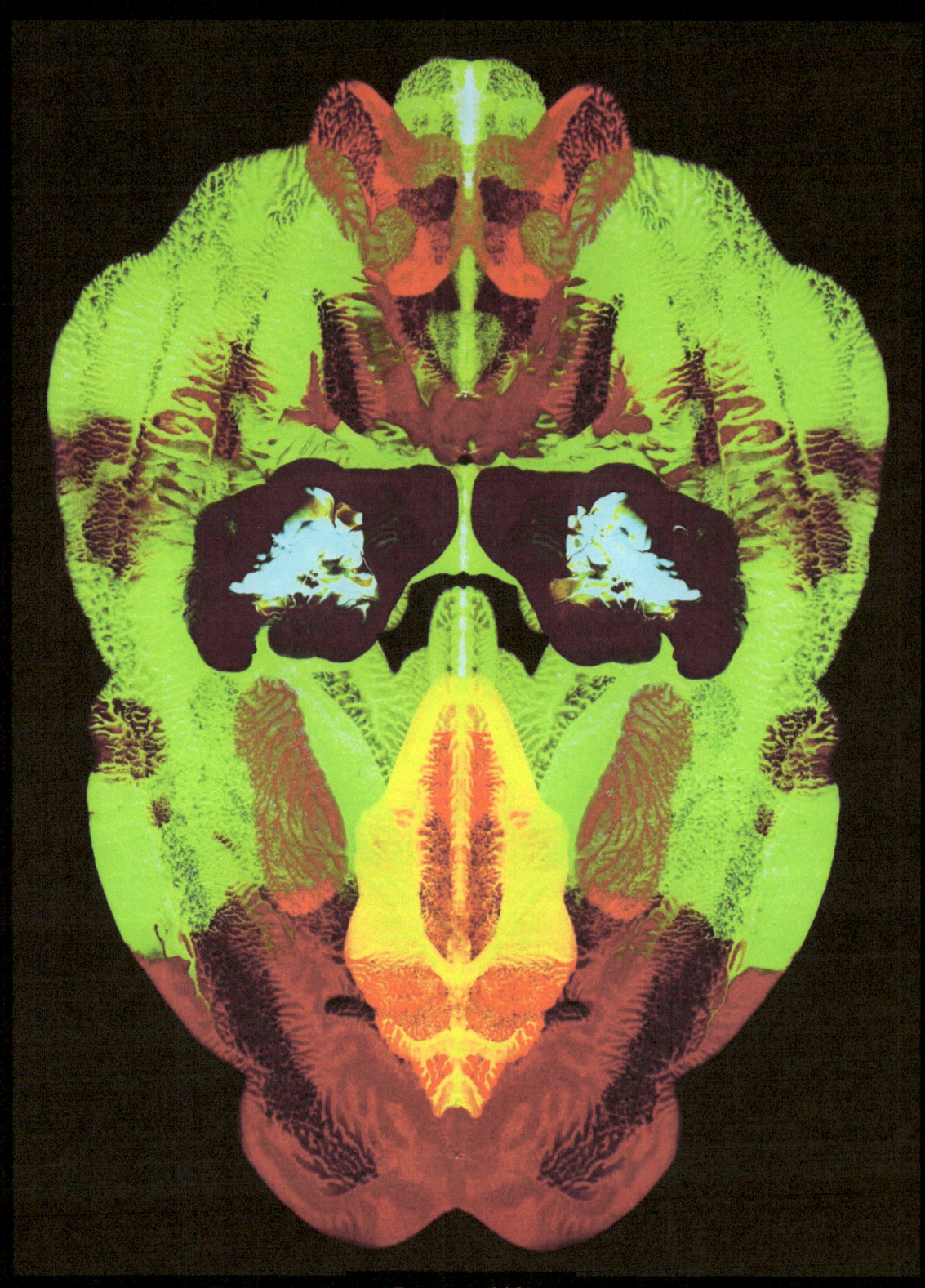

Image 112

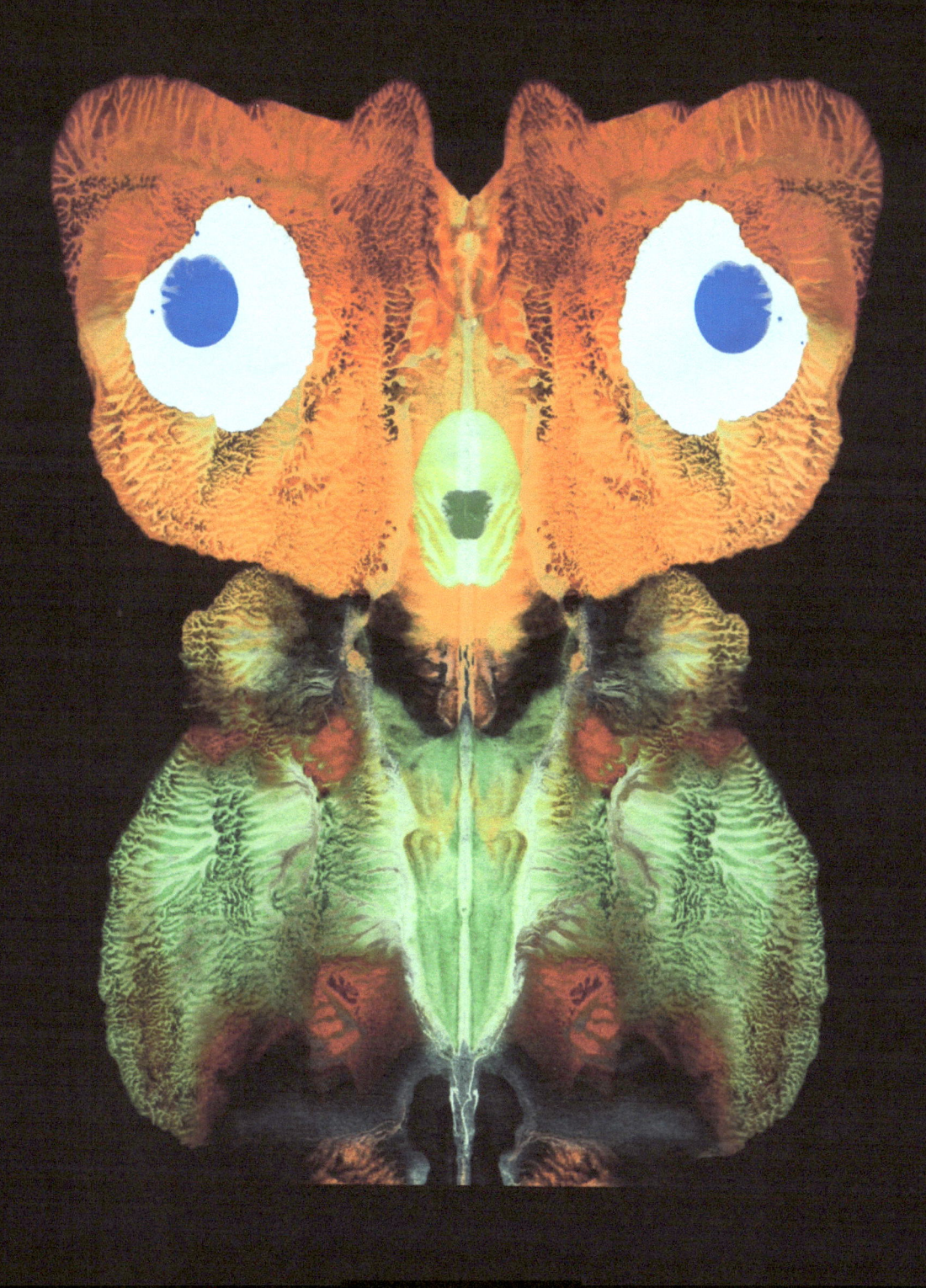

Image 113

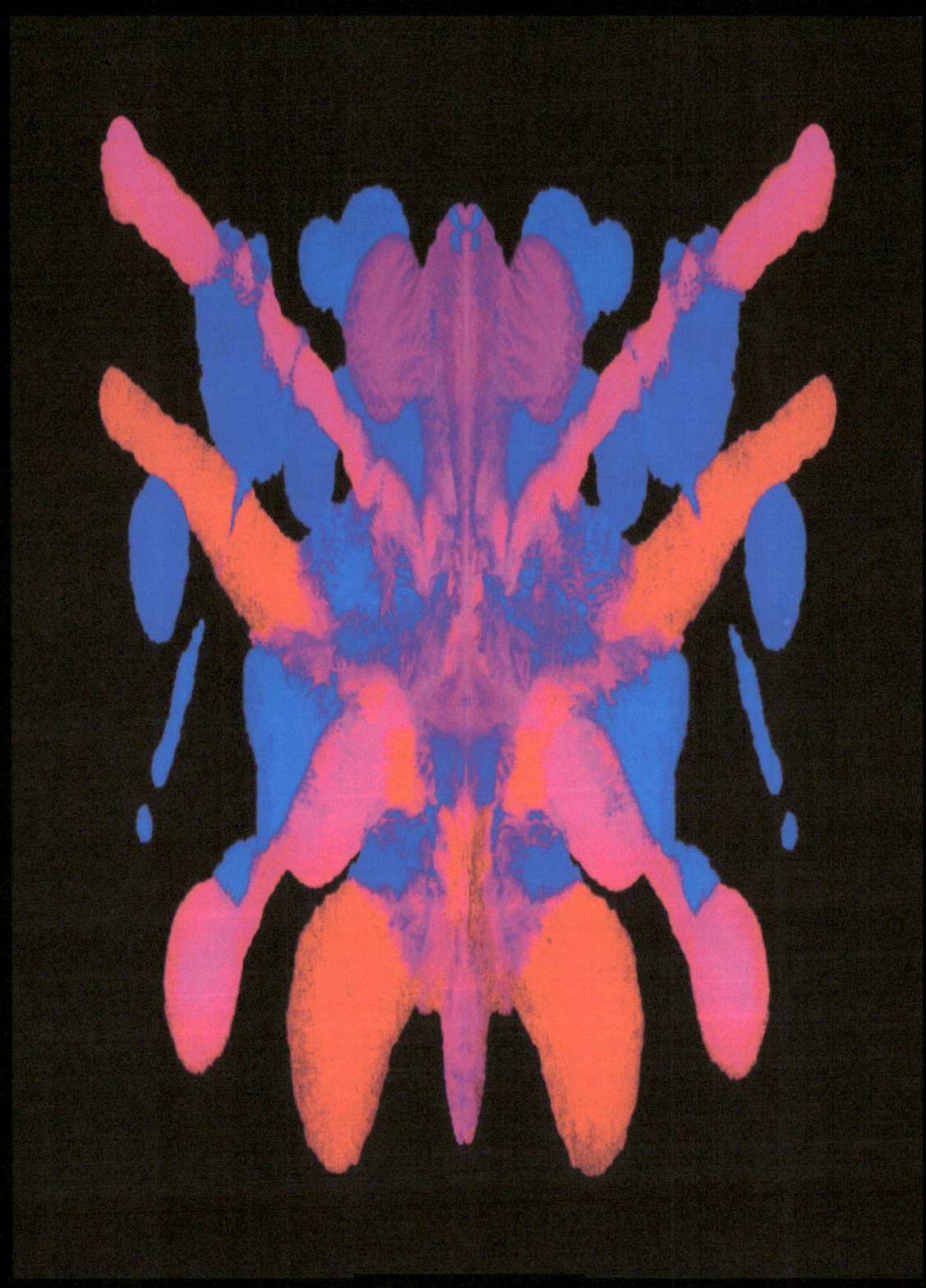

Image 114

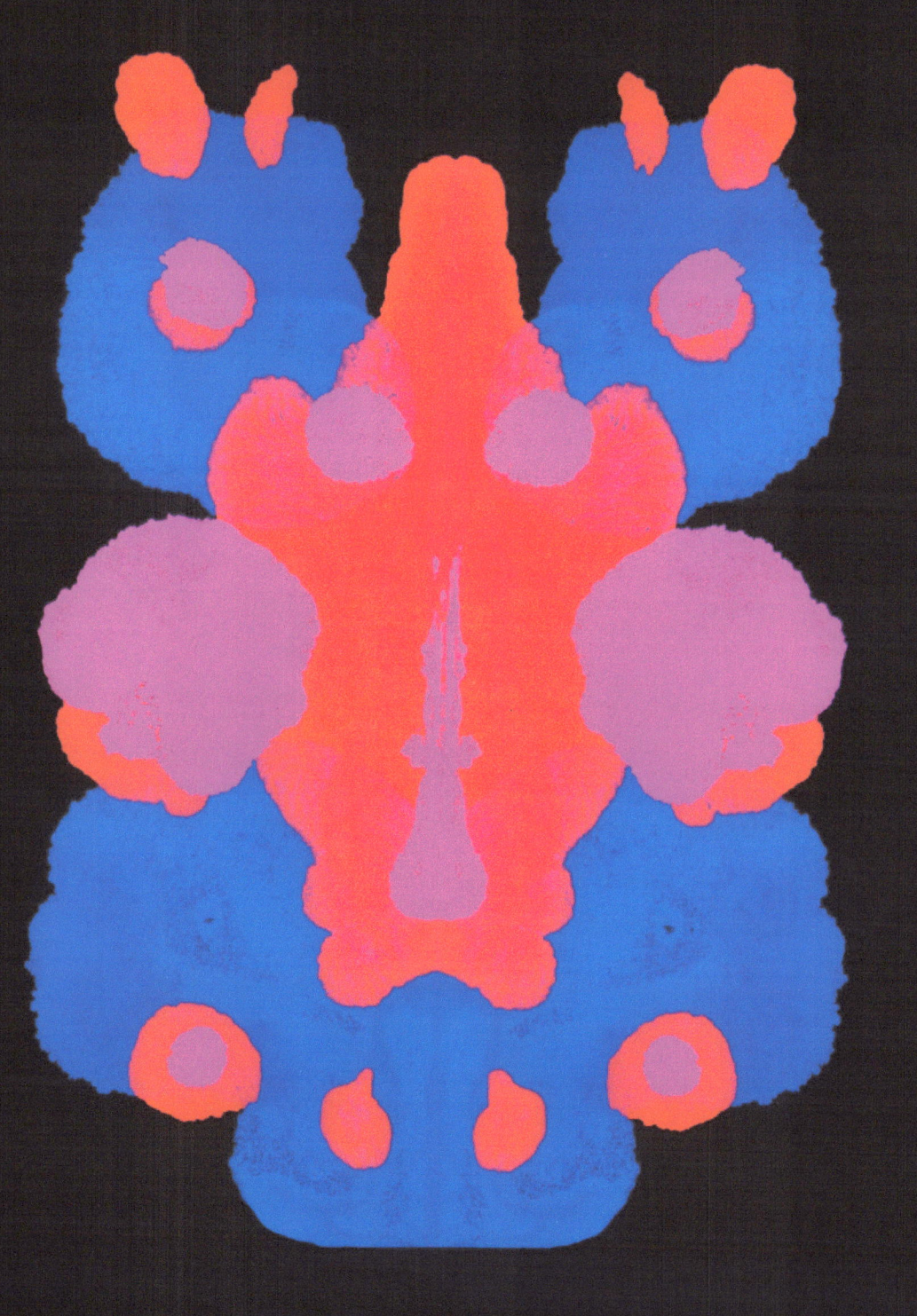

Image 115

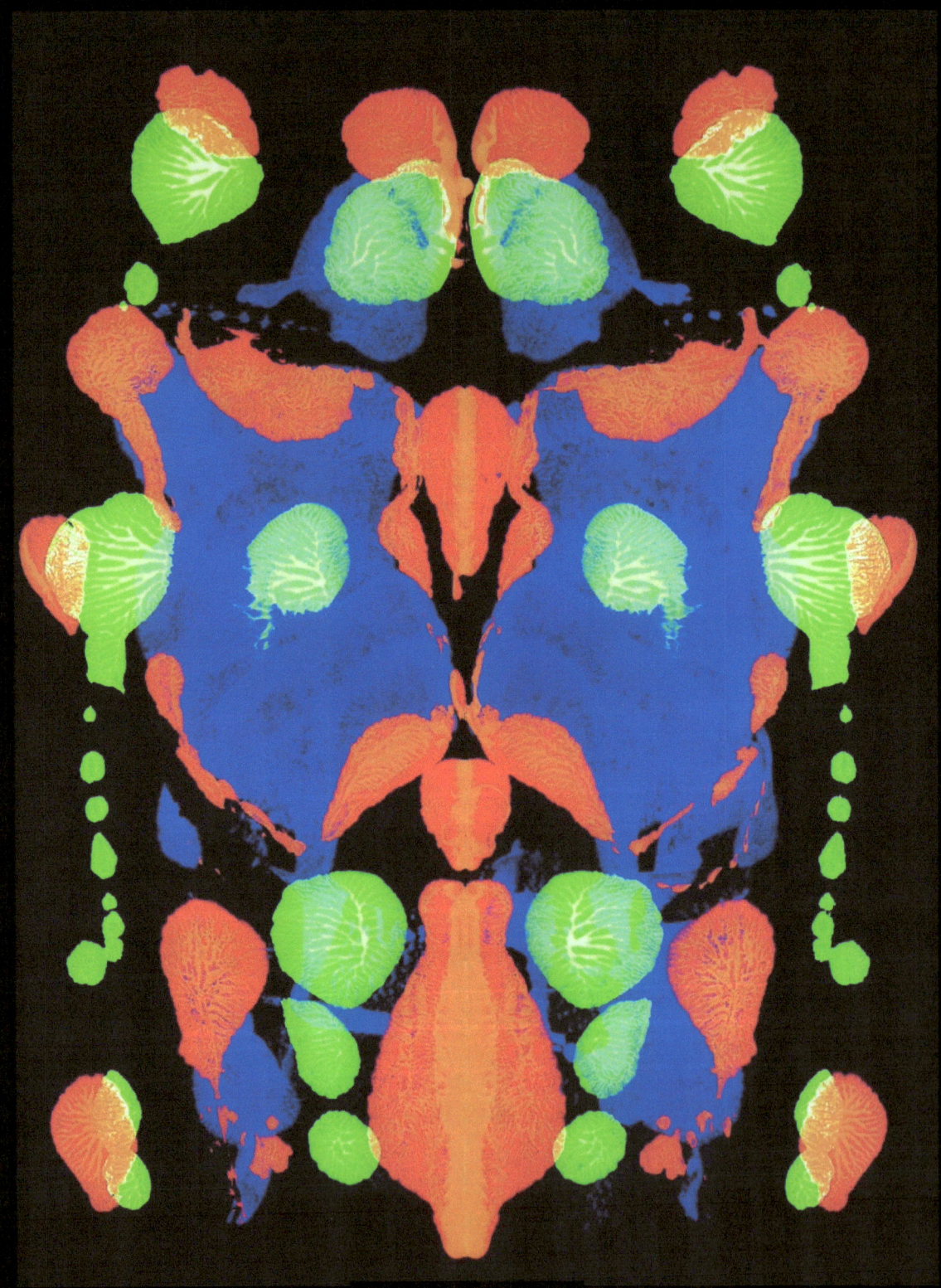

Image 116

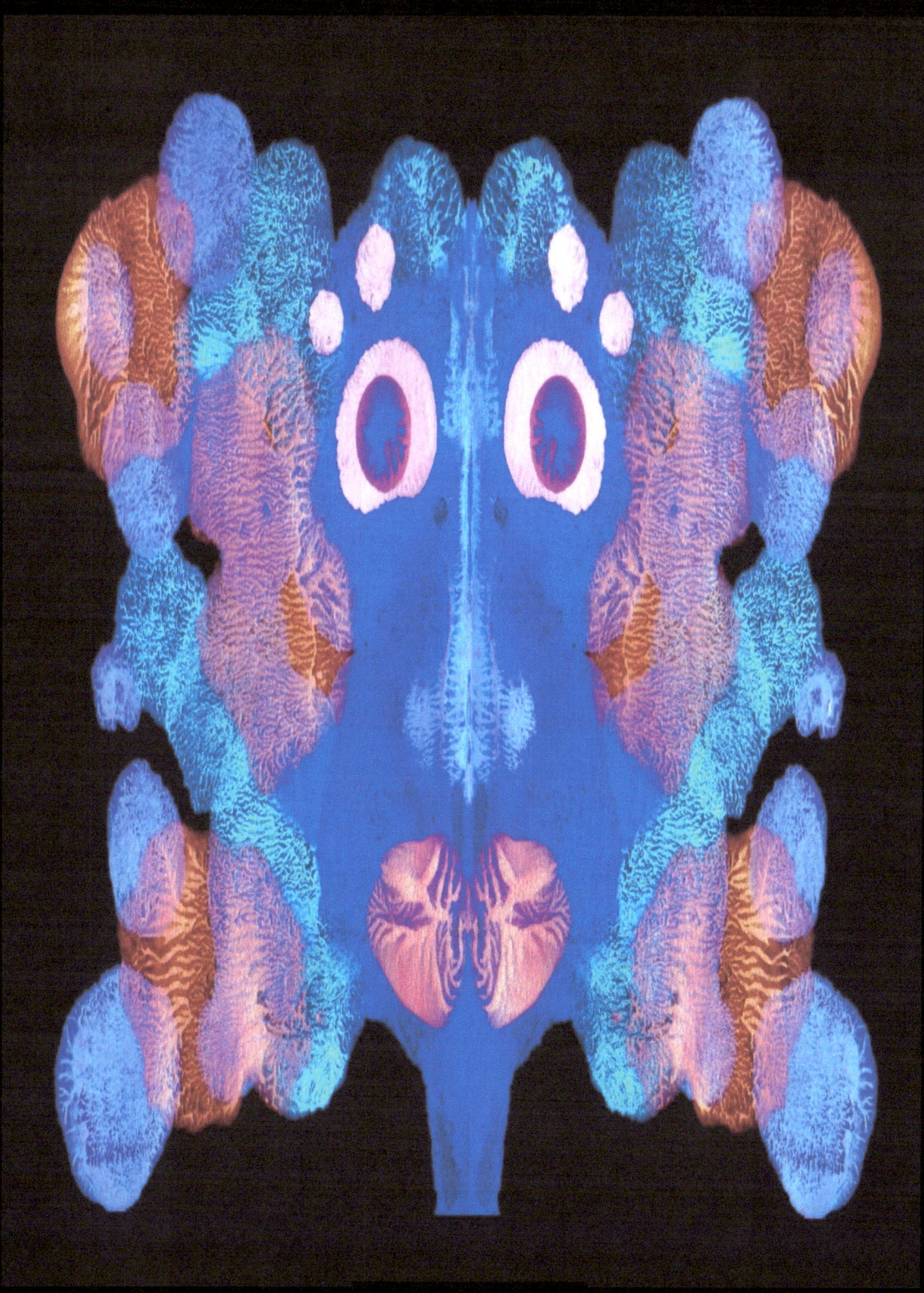

Image 117

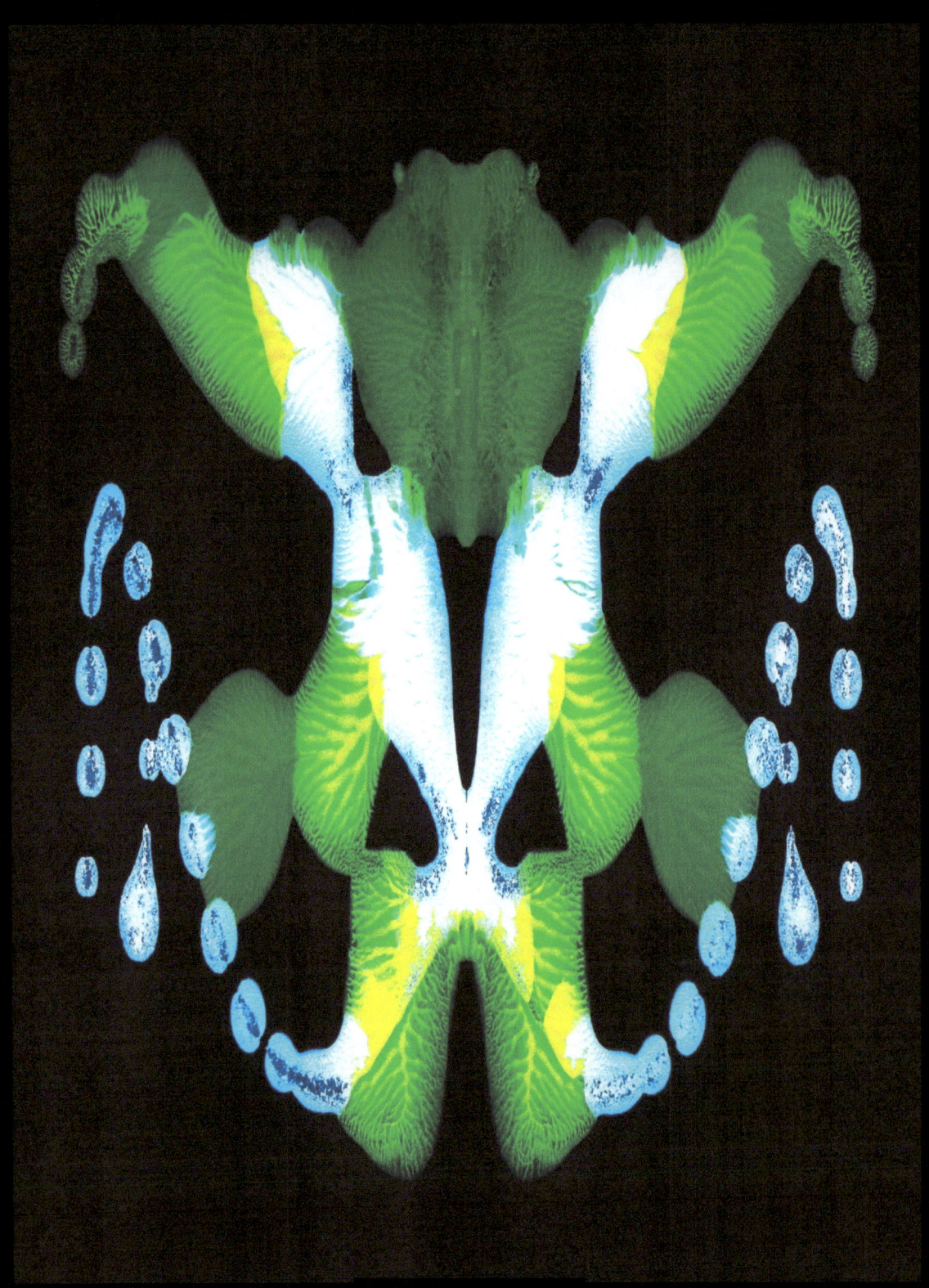

Image 118

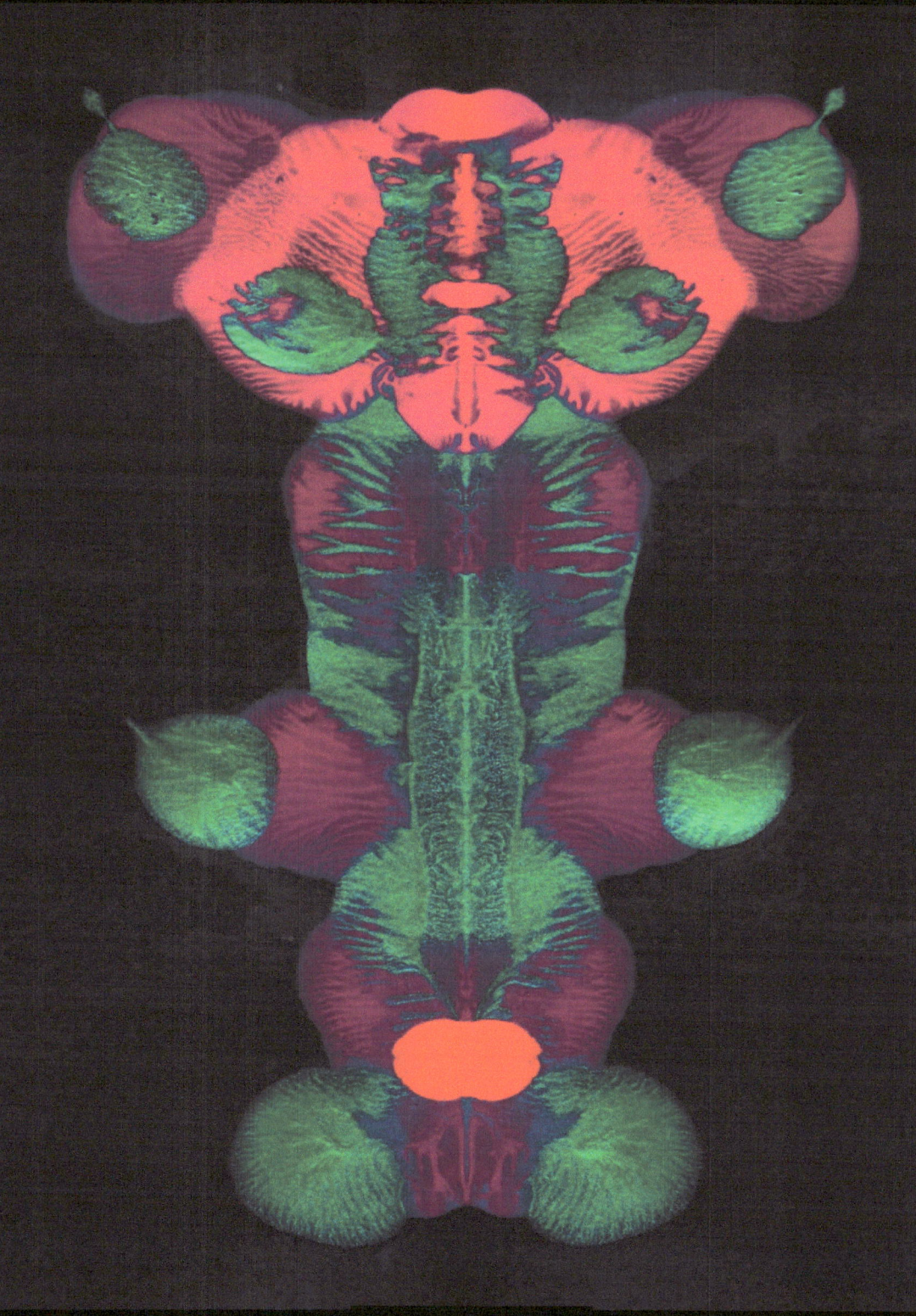

Image 119

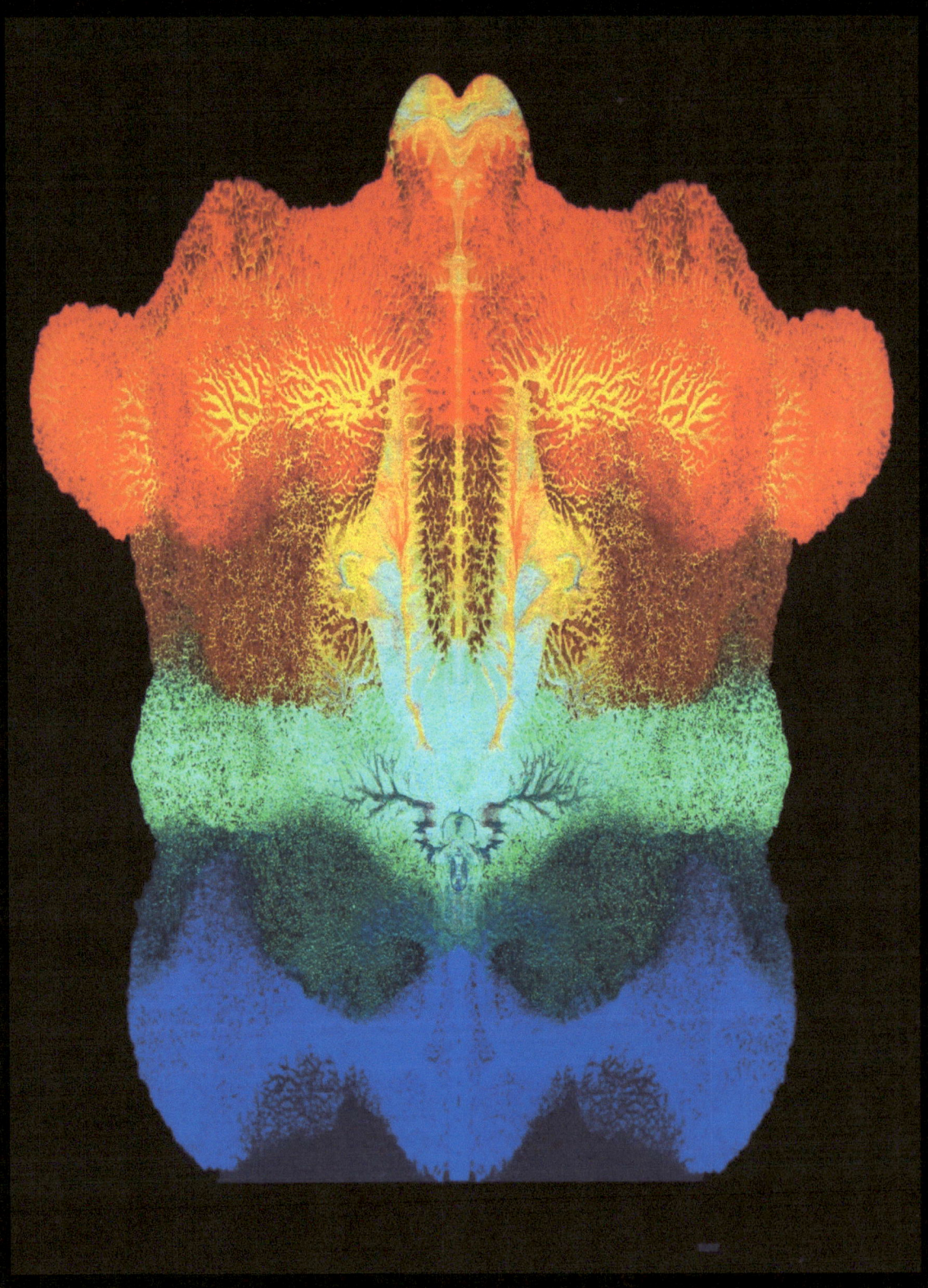

Image 120

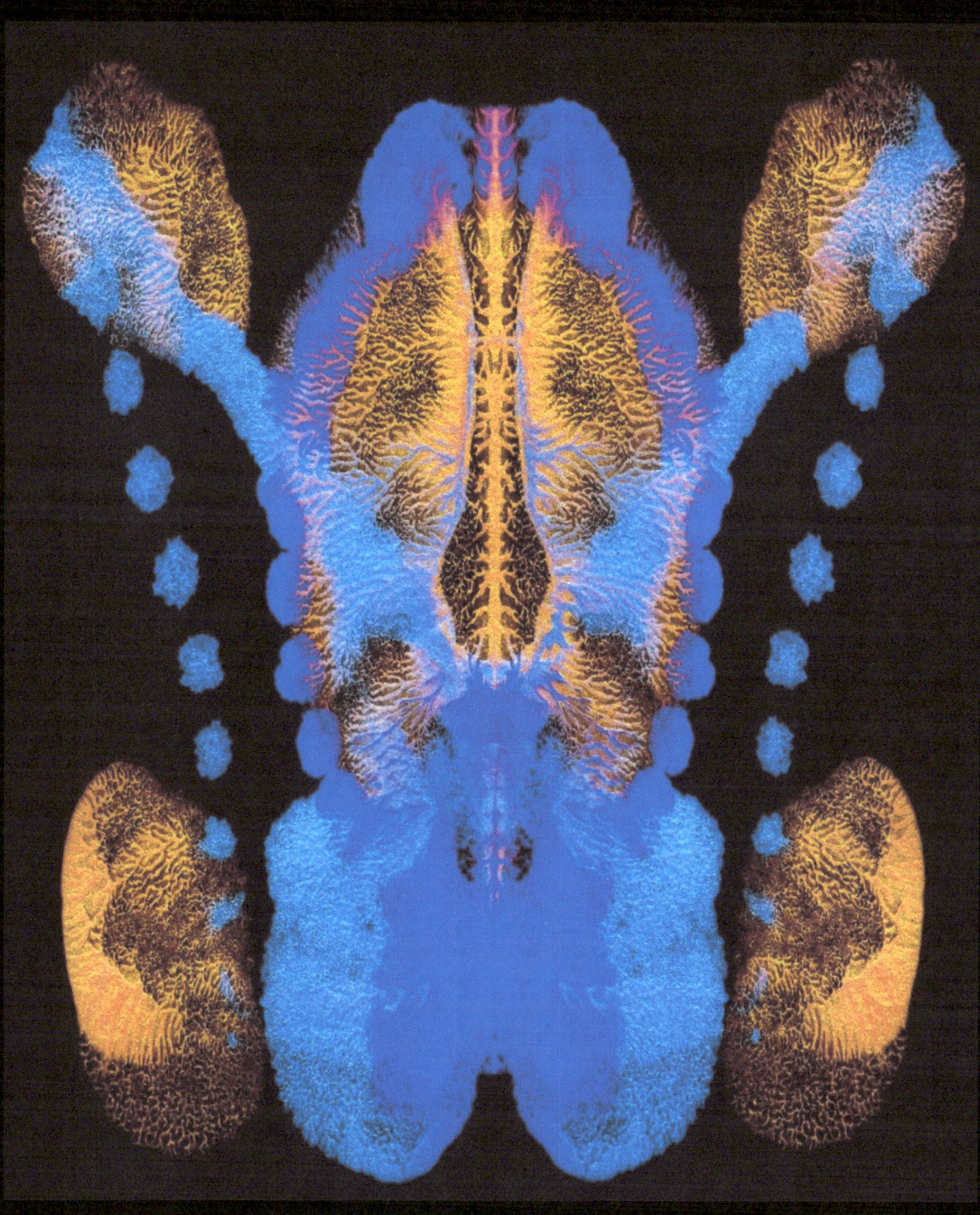

Image 121

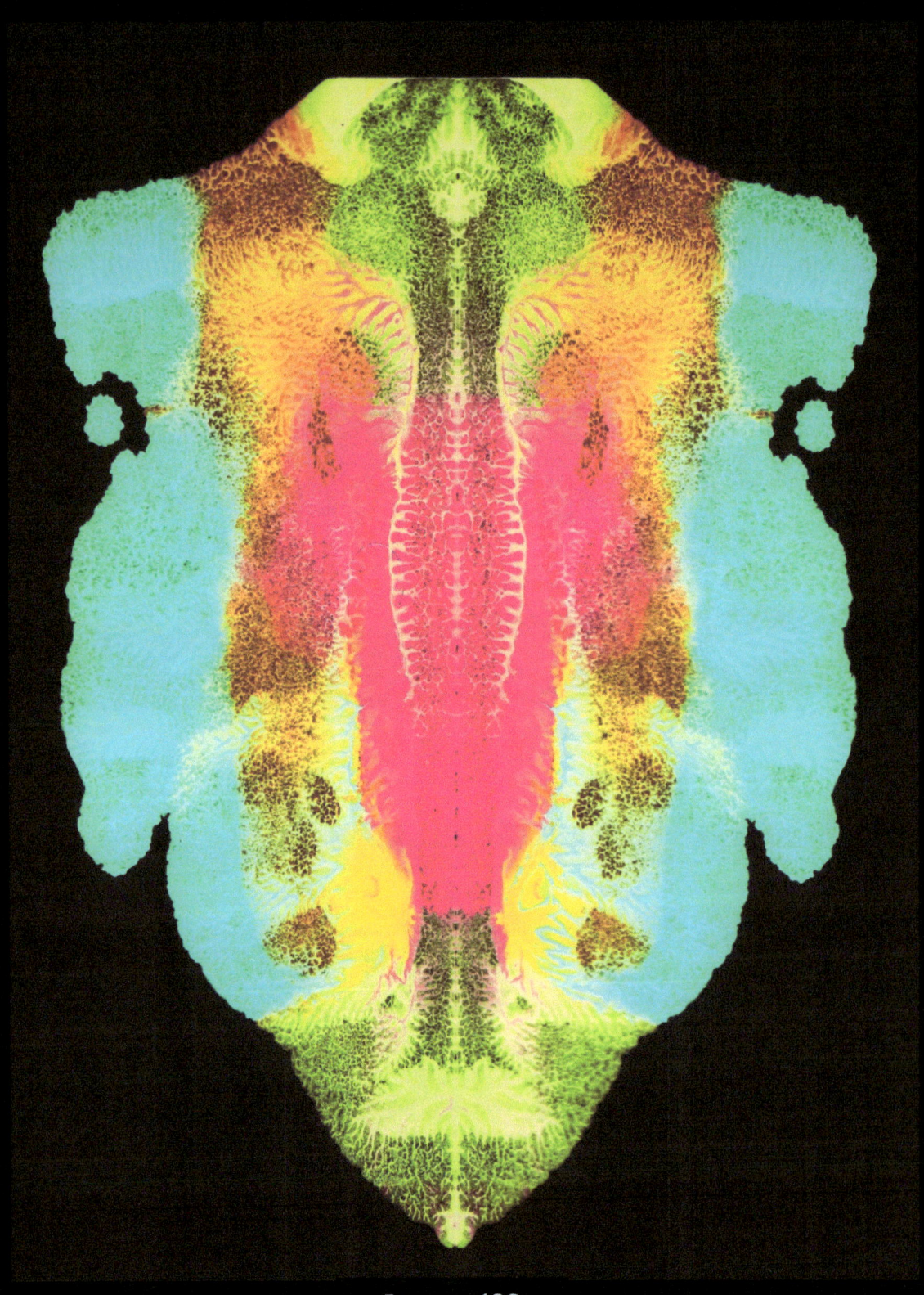

Image 122

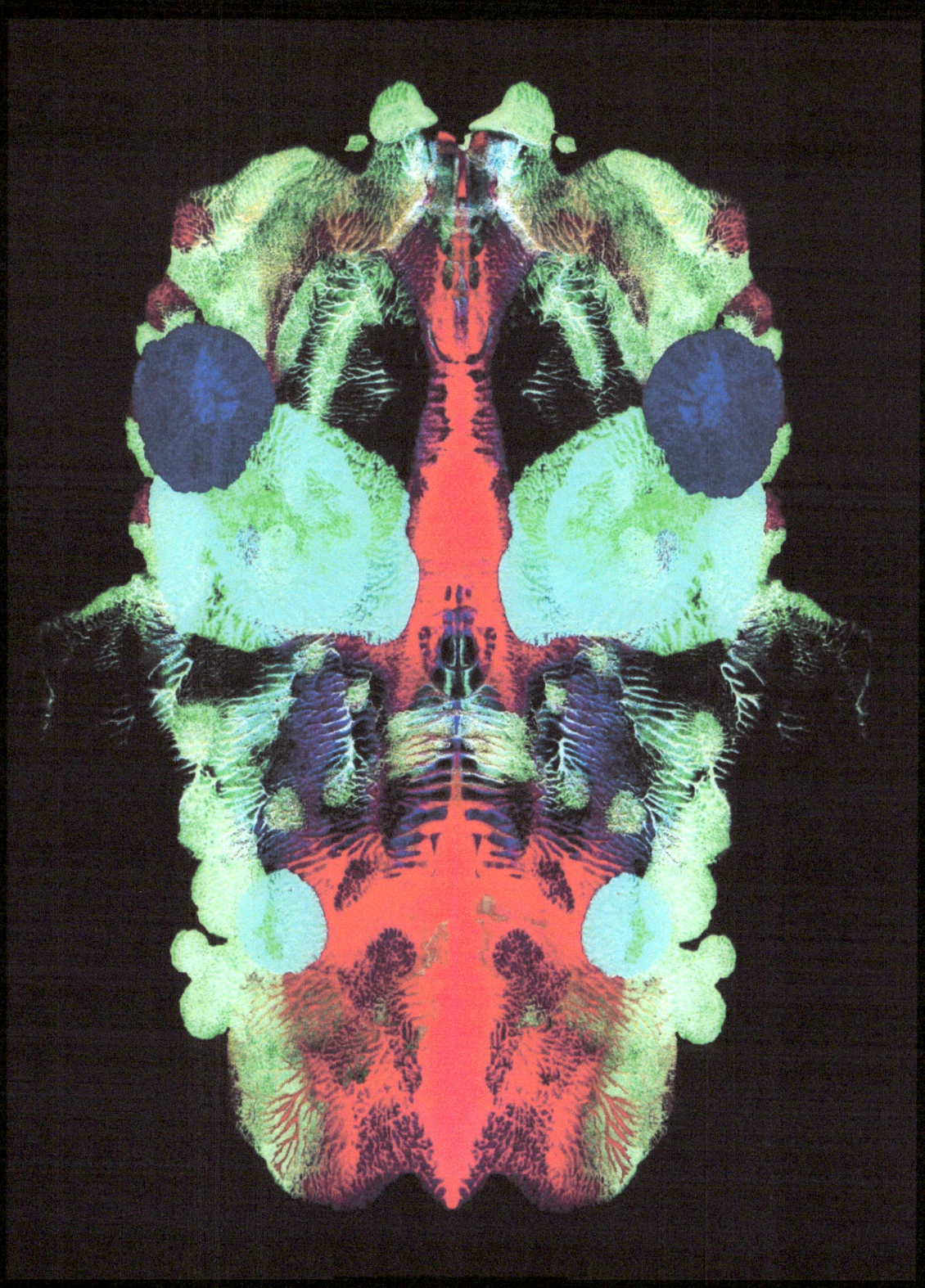

Image 123

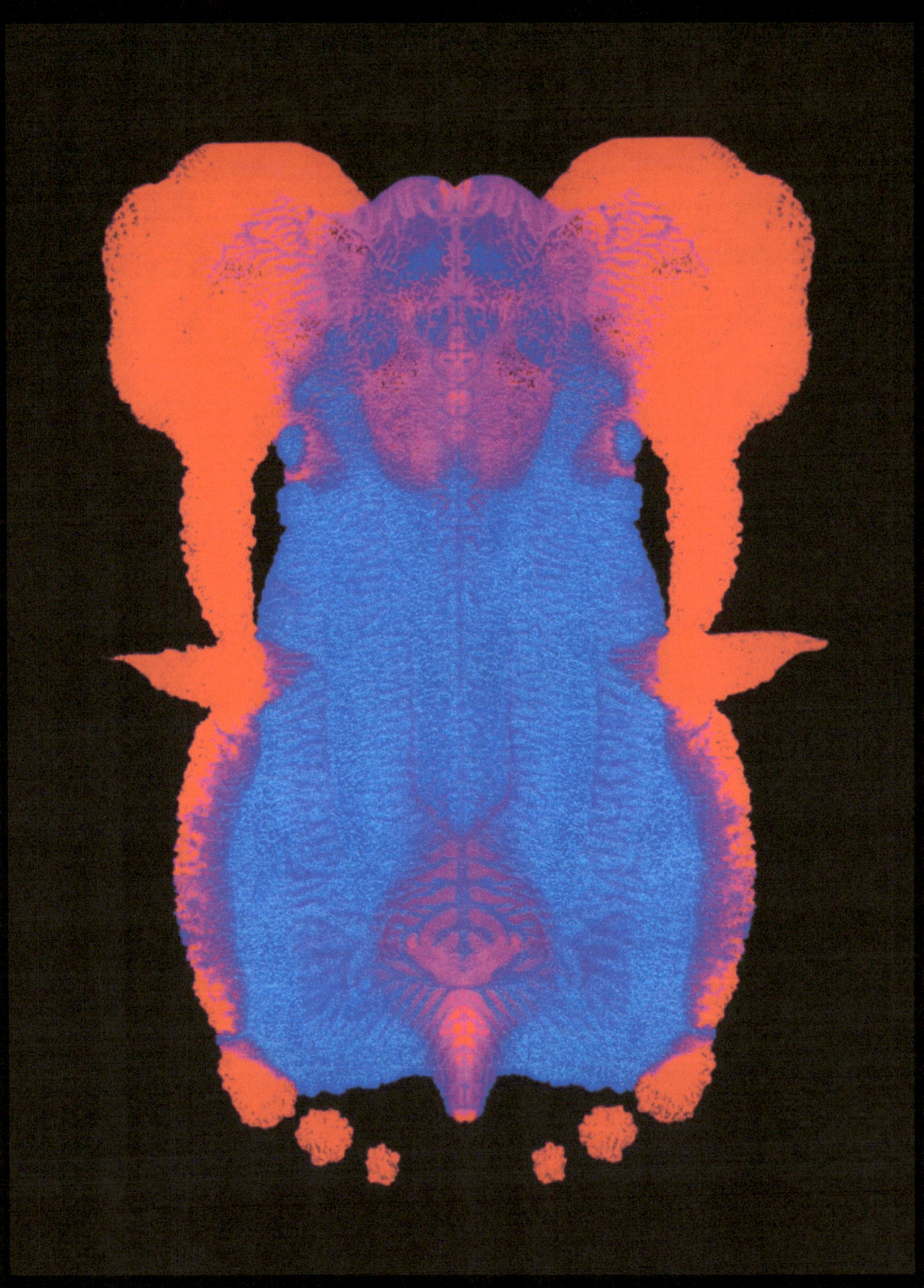
Image 124

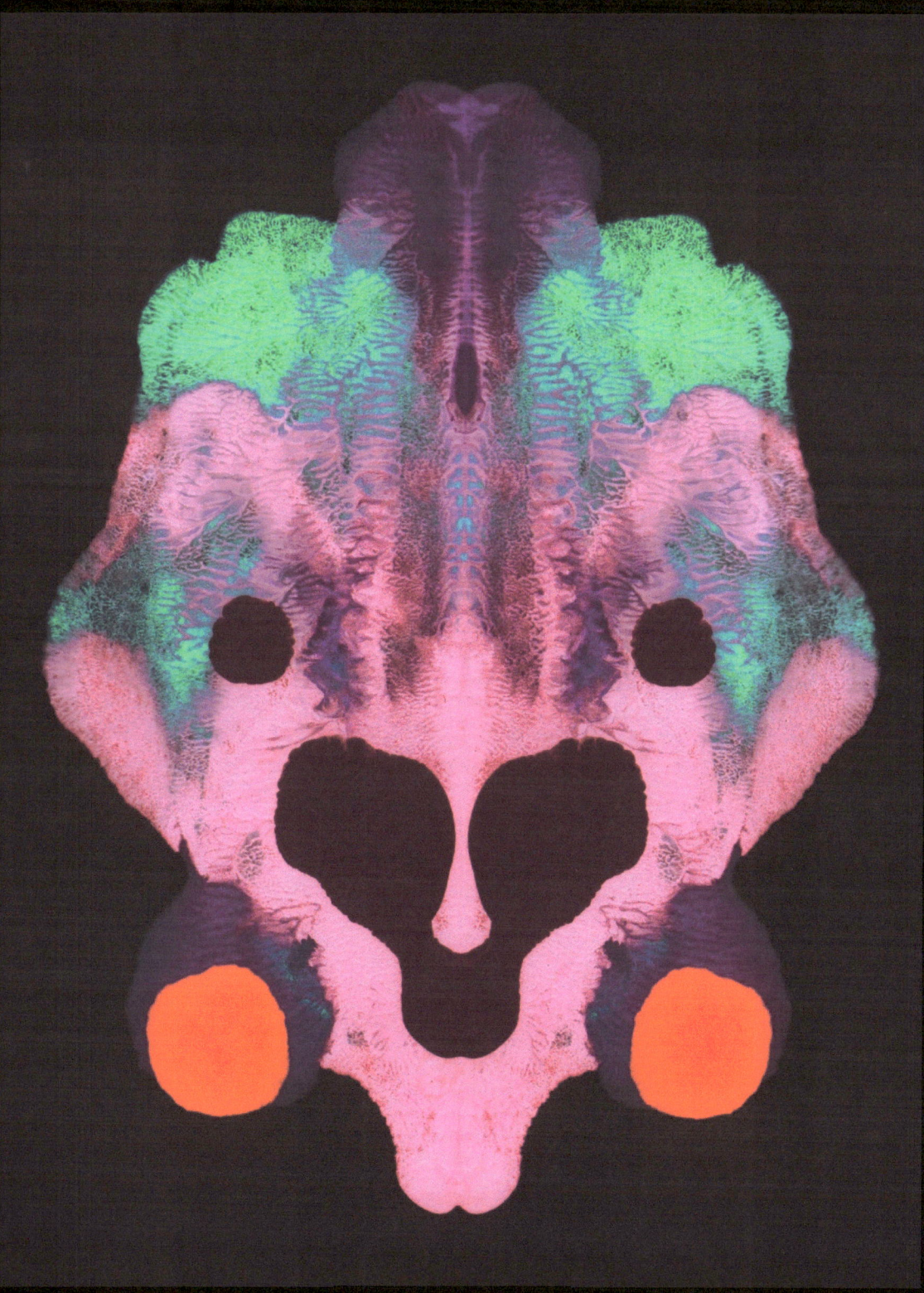

Image 125

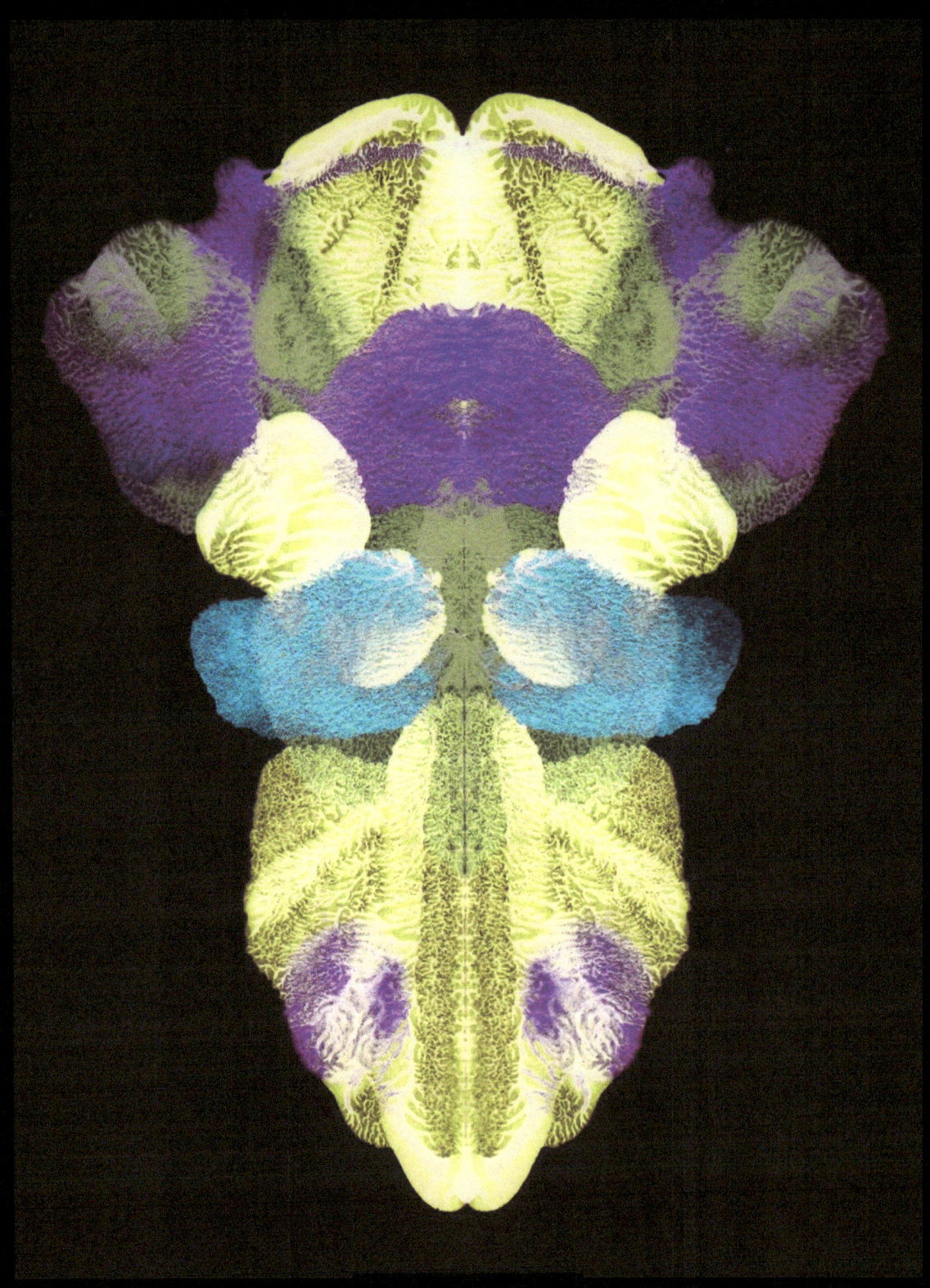

Image 126

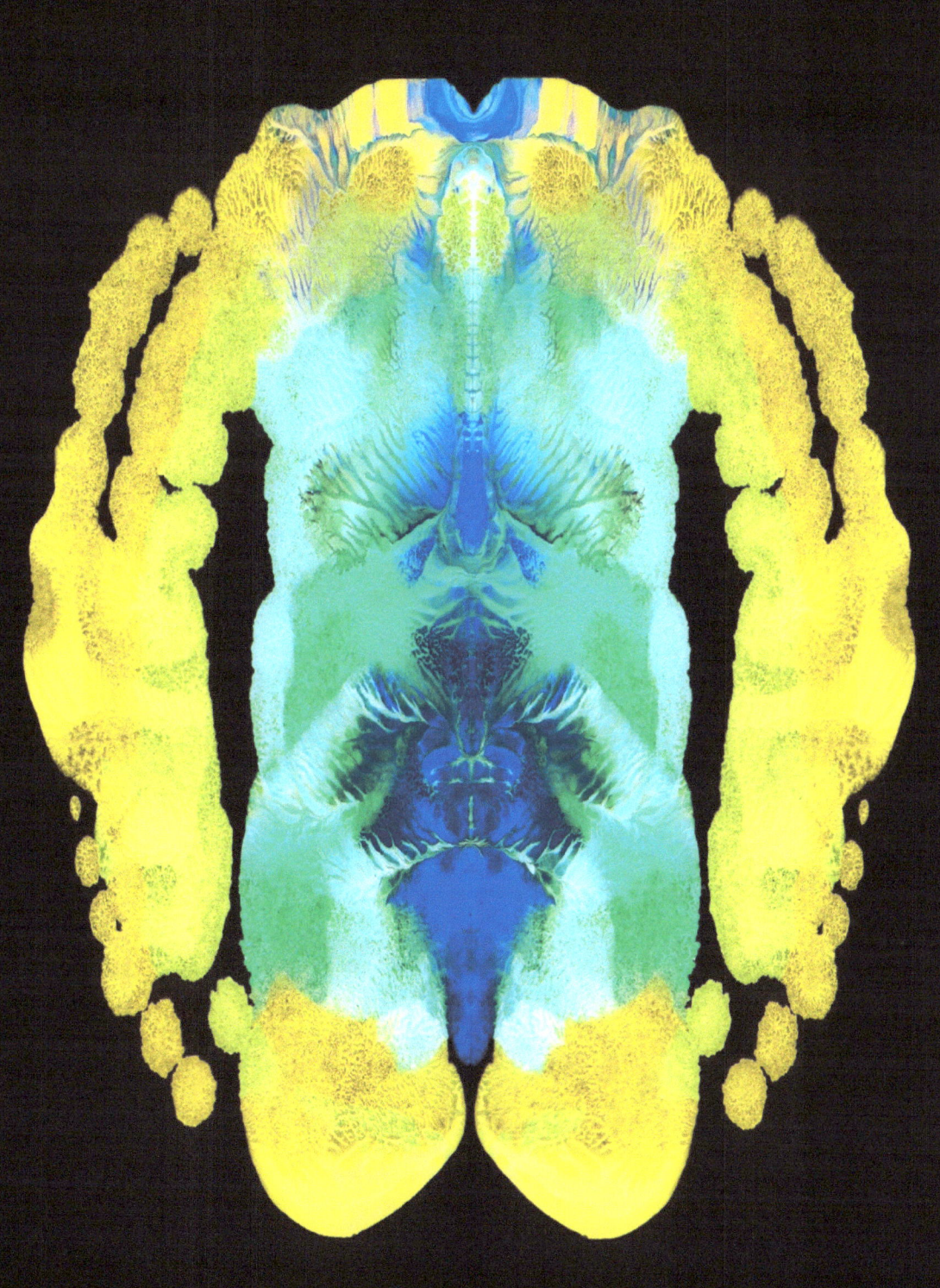

Image 127

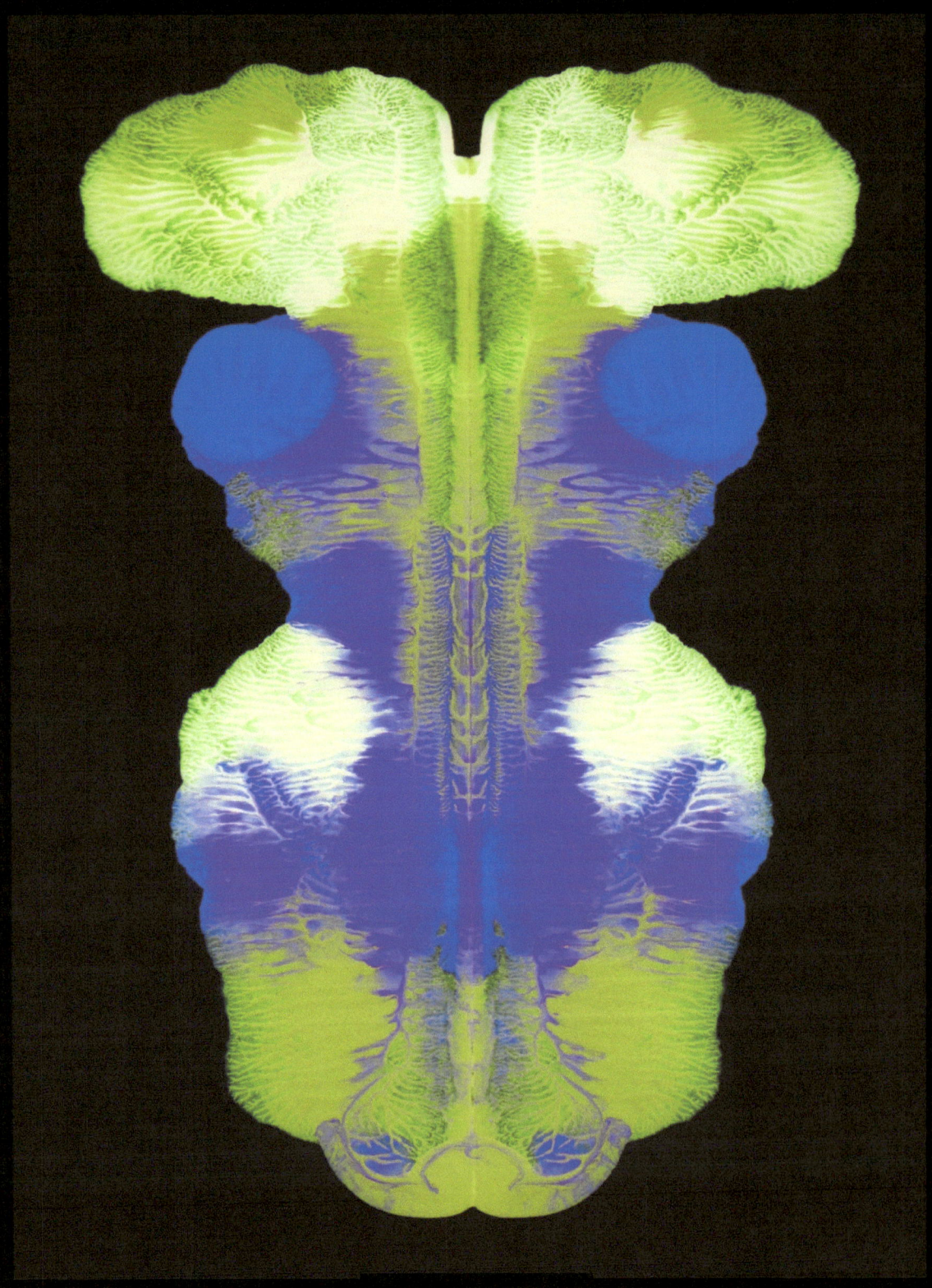

Image 128

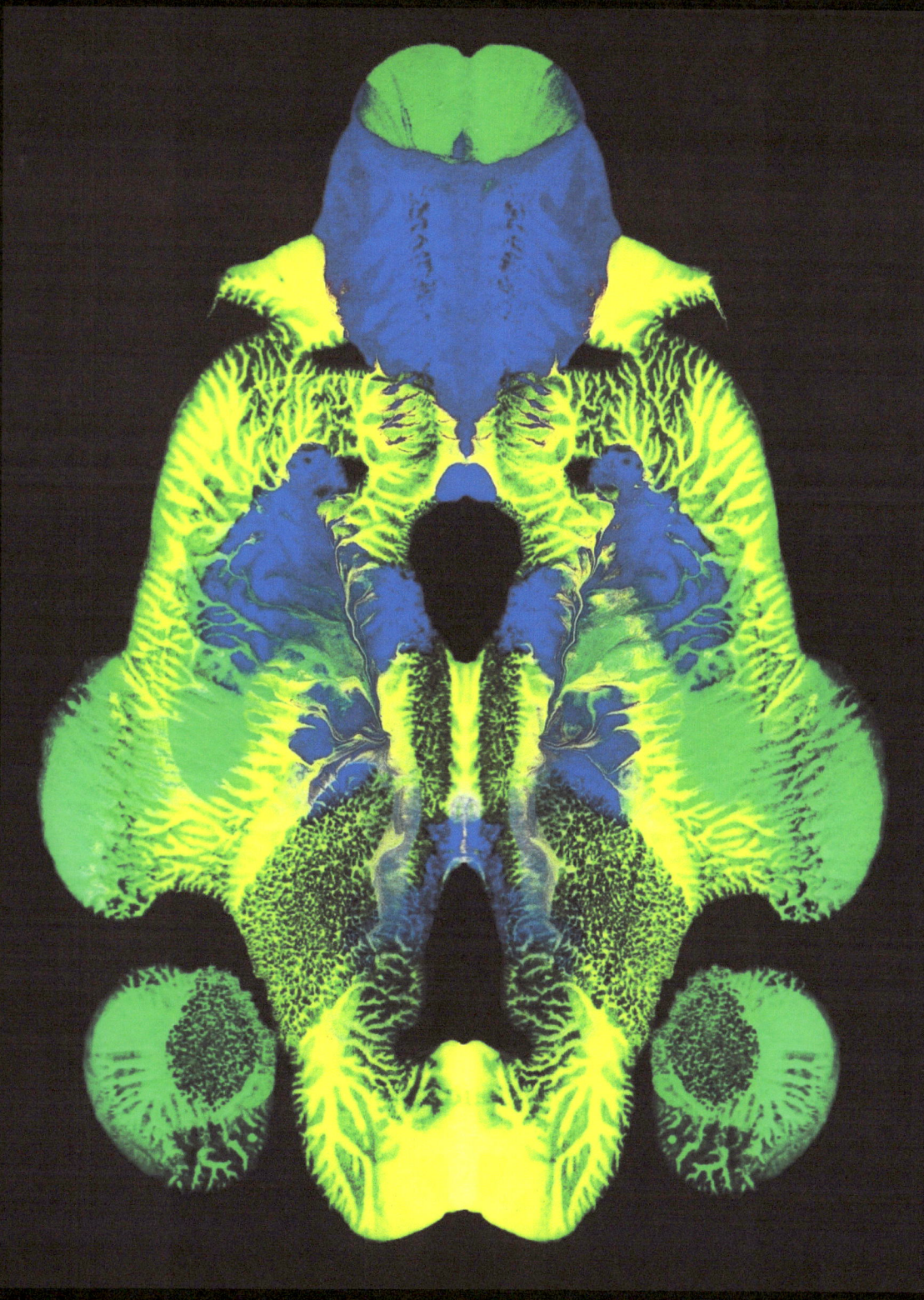

Image 129

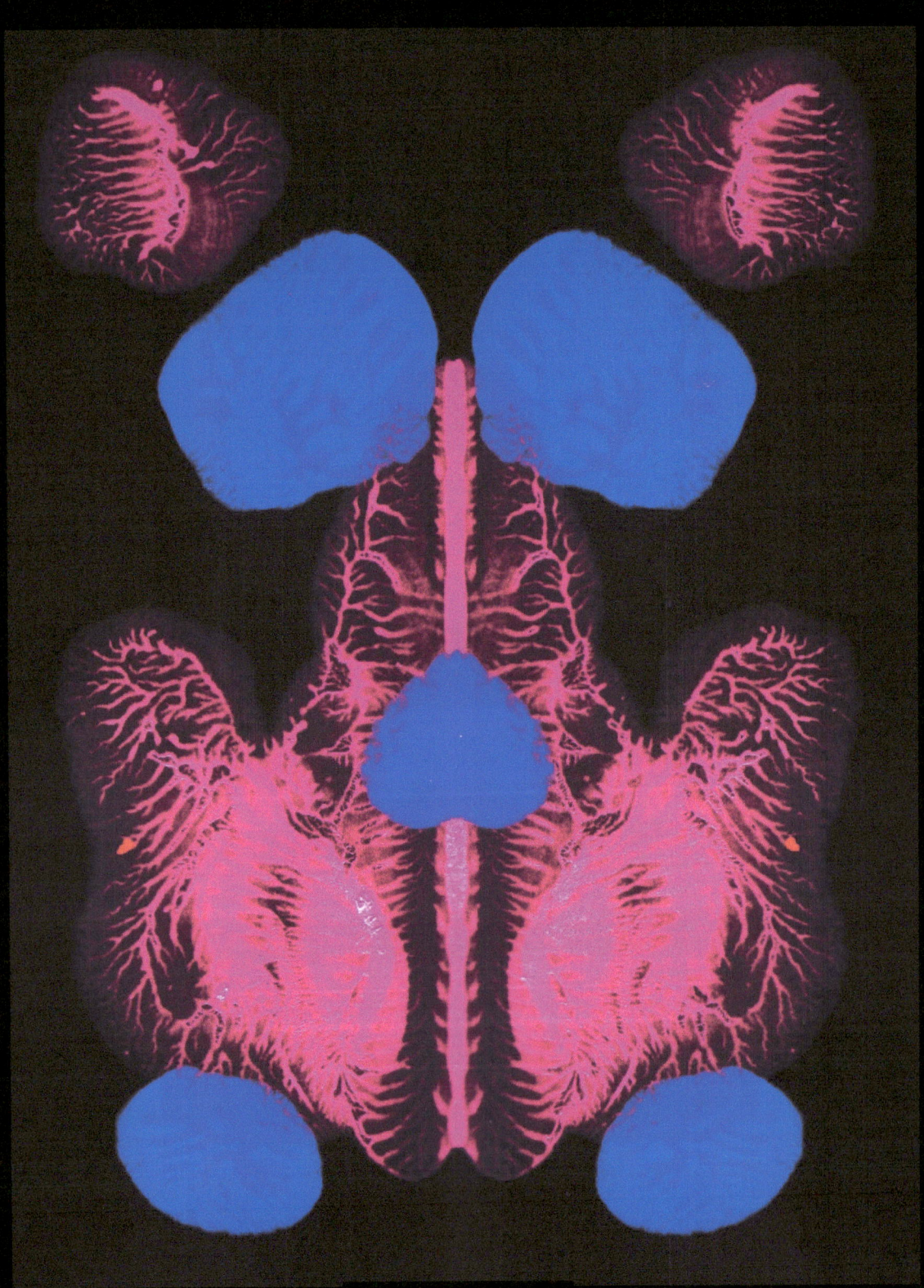

Image 130

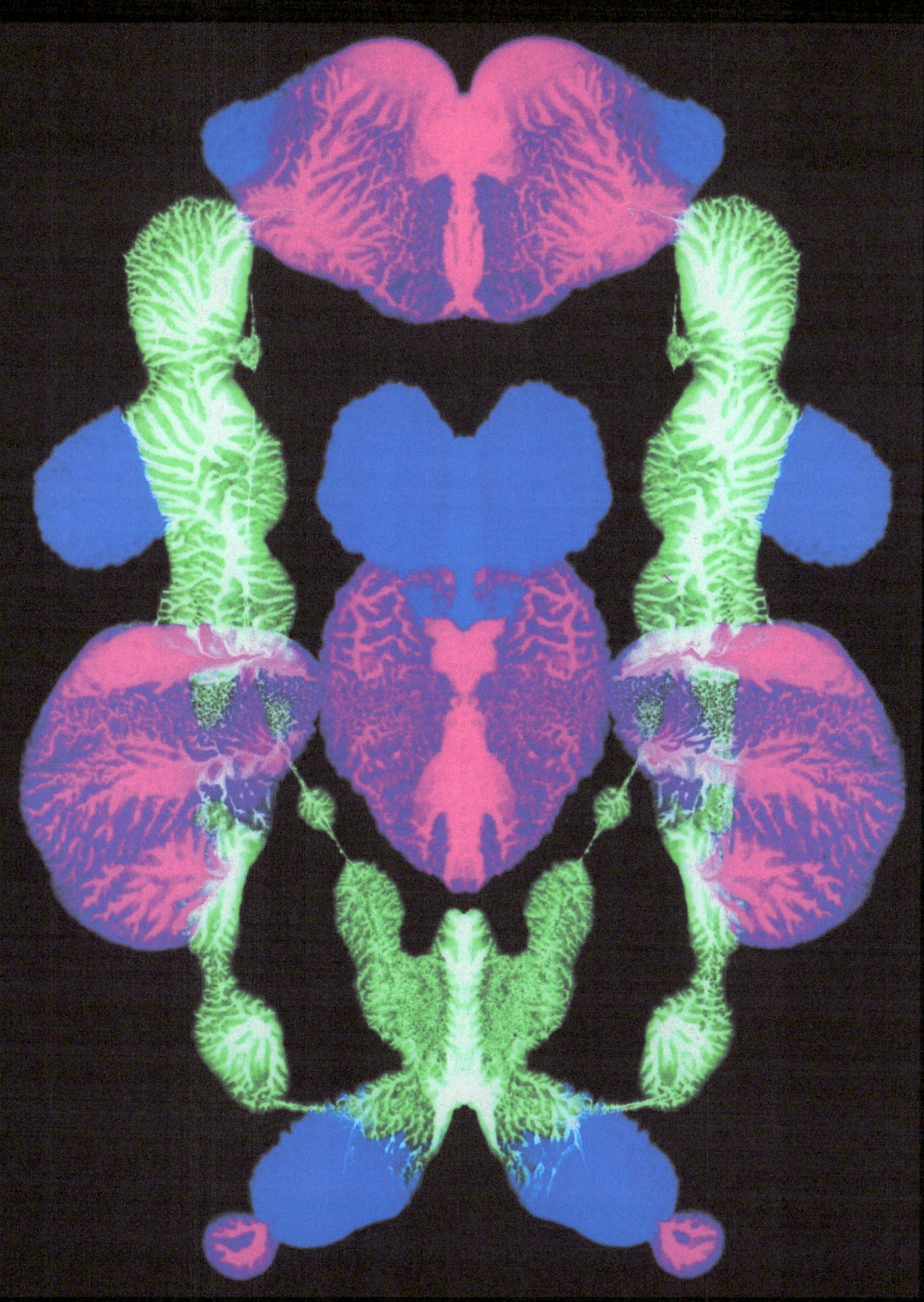

Image 131

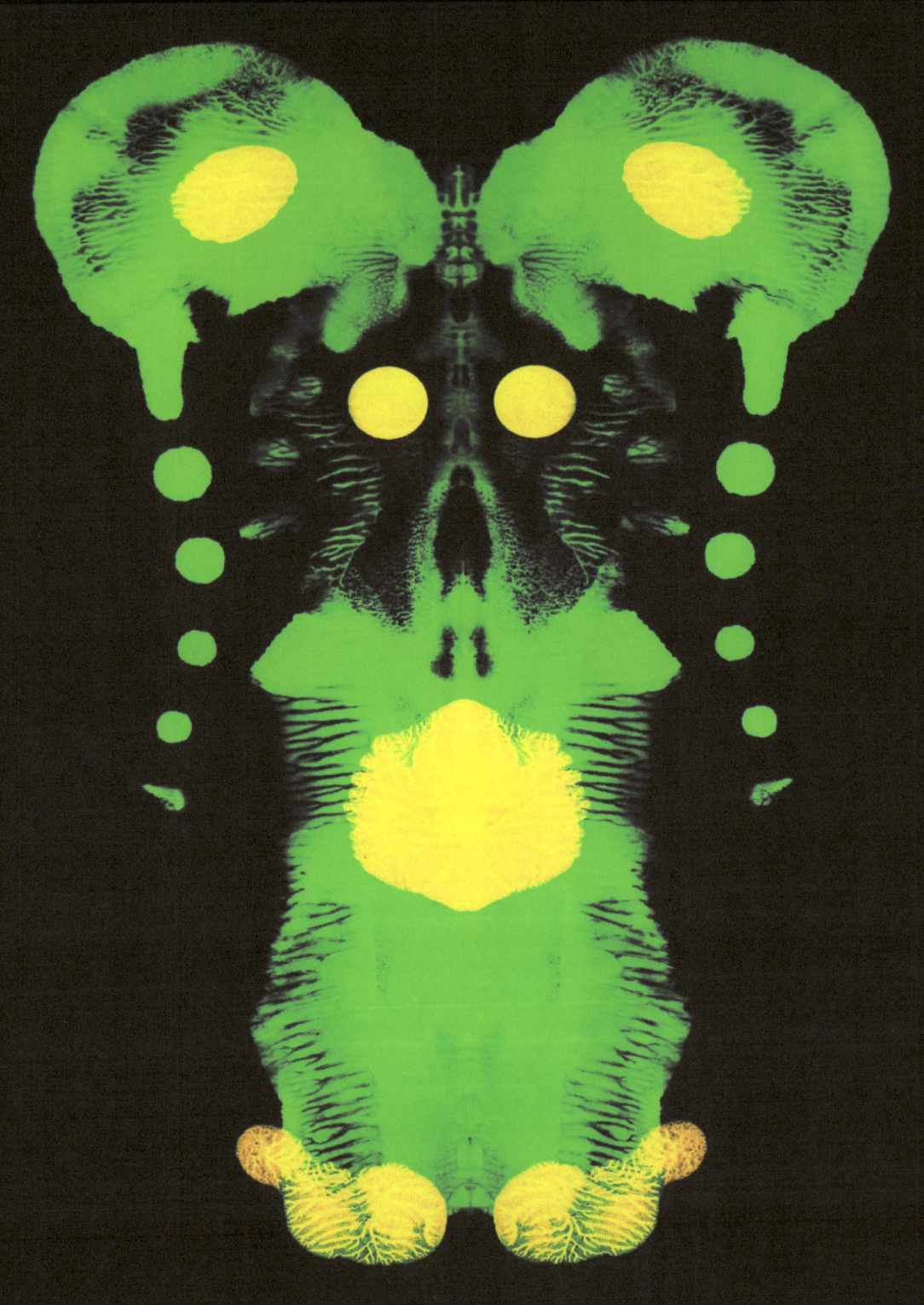

Image 132

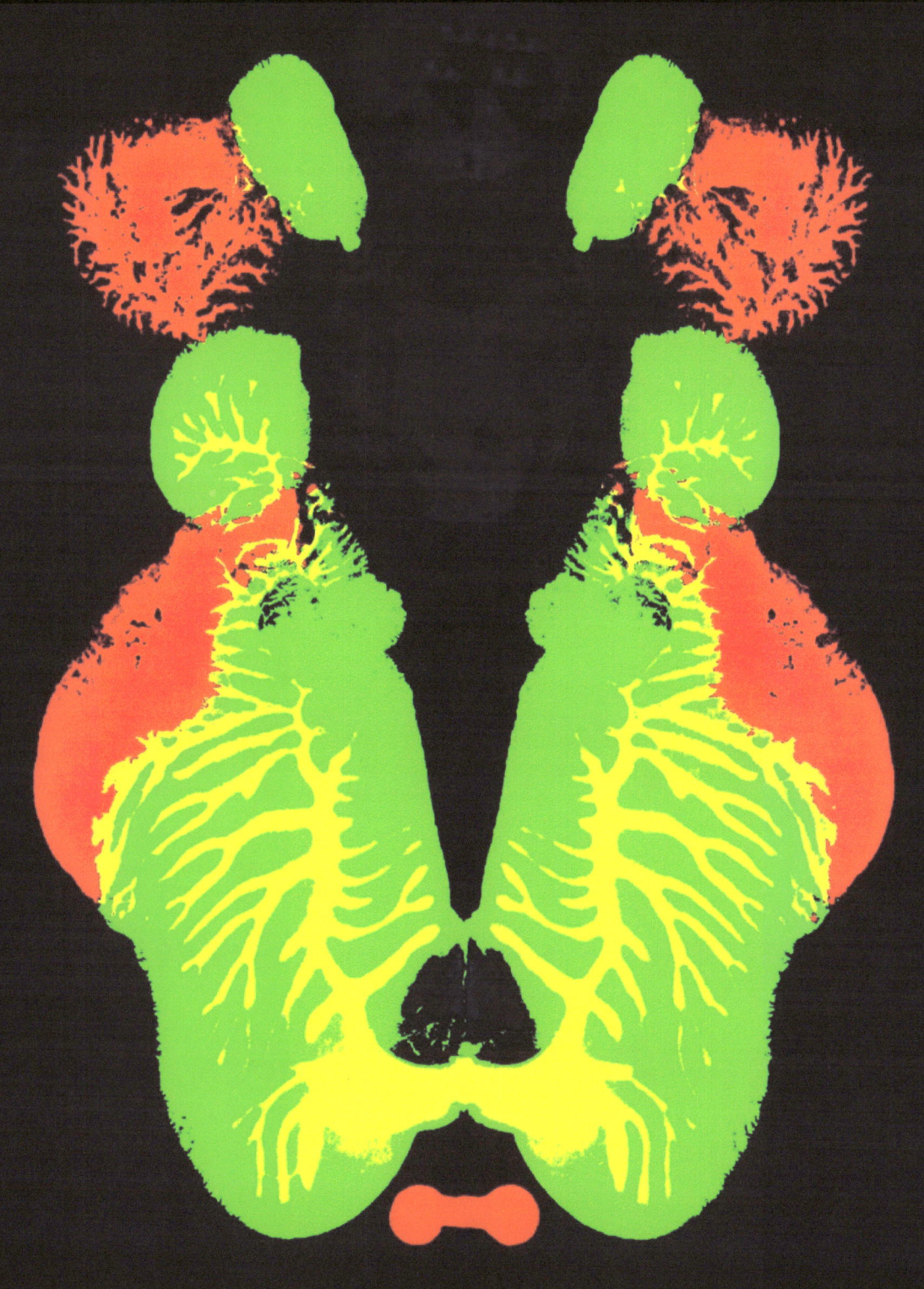

Image 133

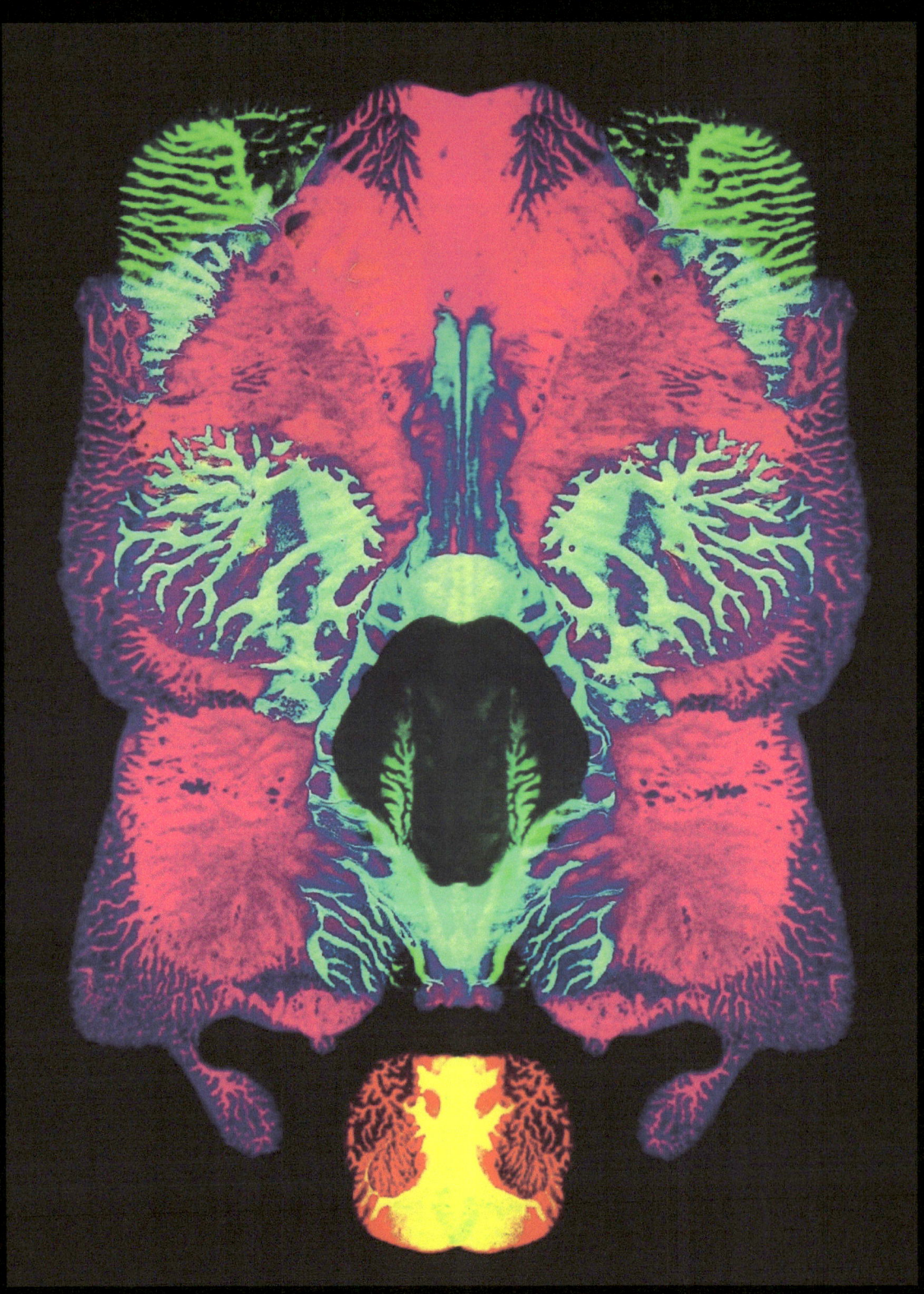

Image 134

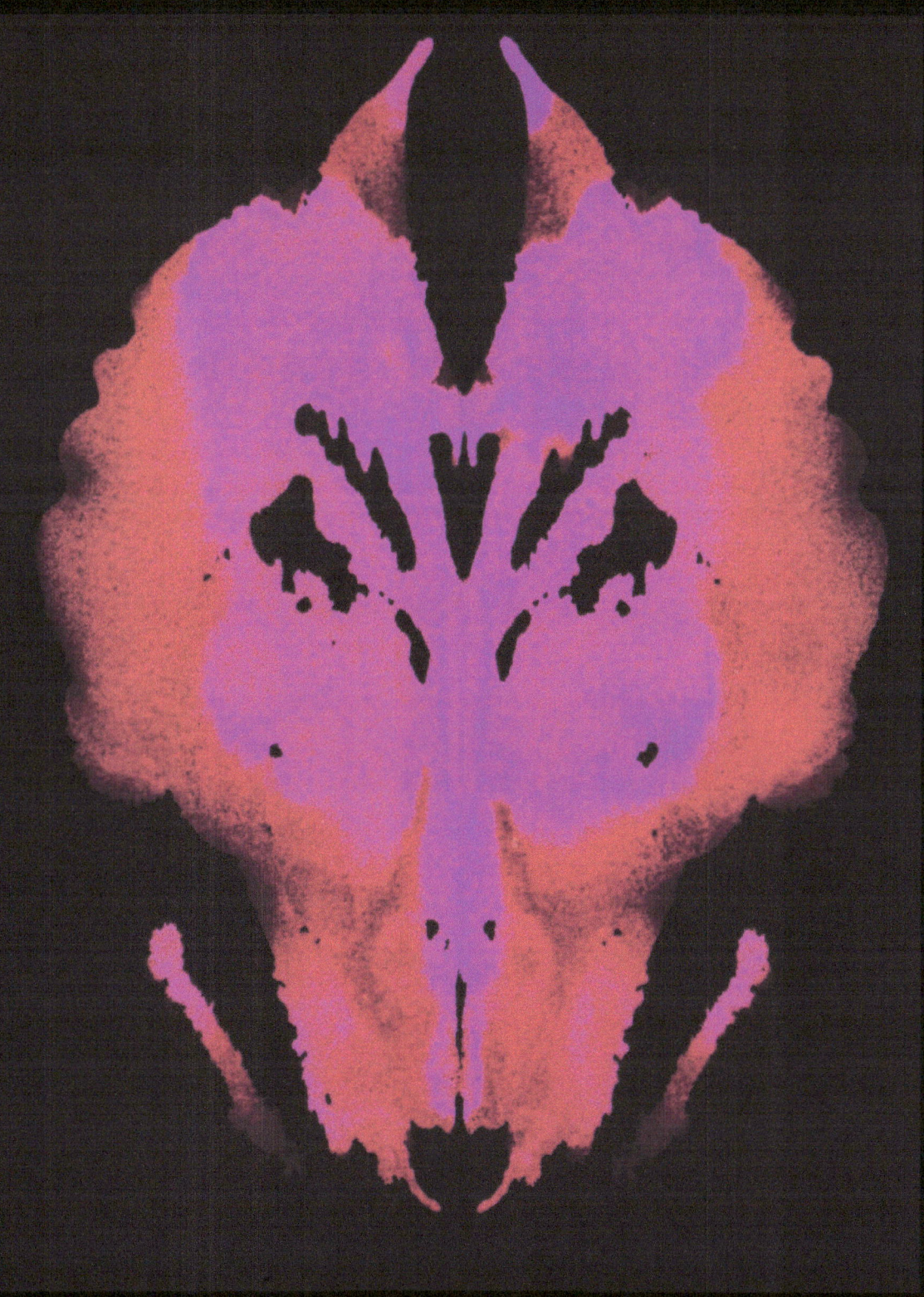

Image 135

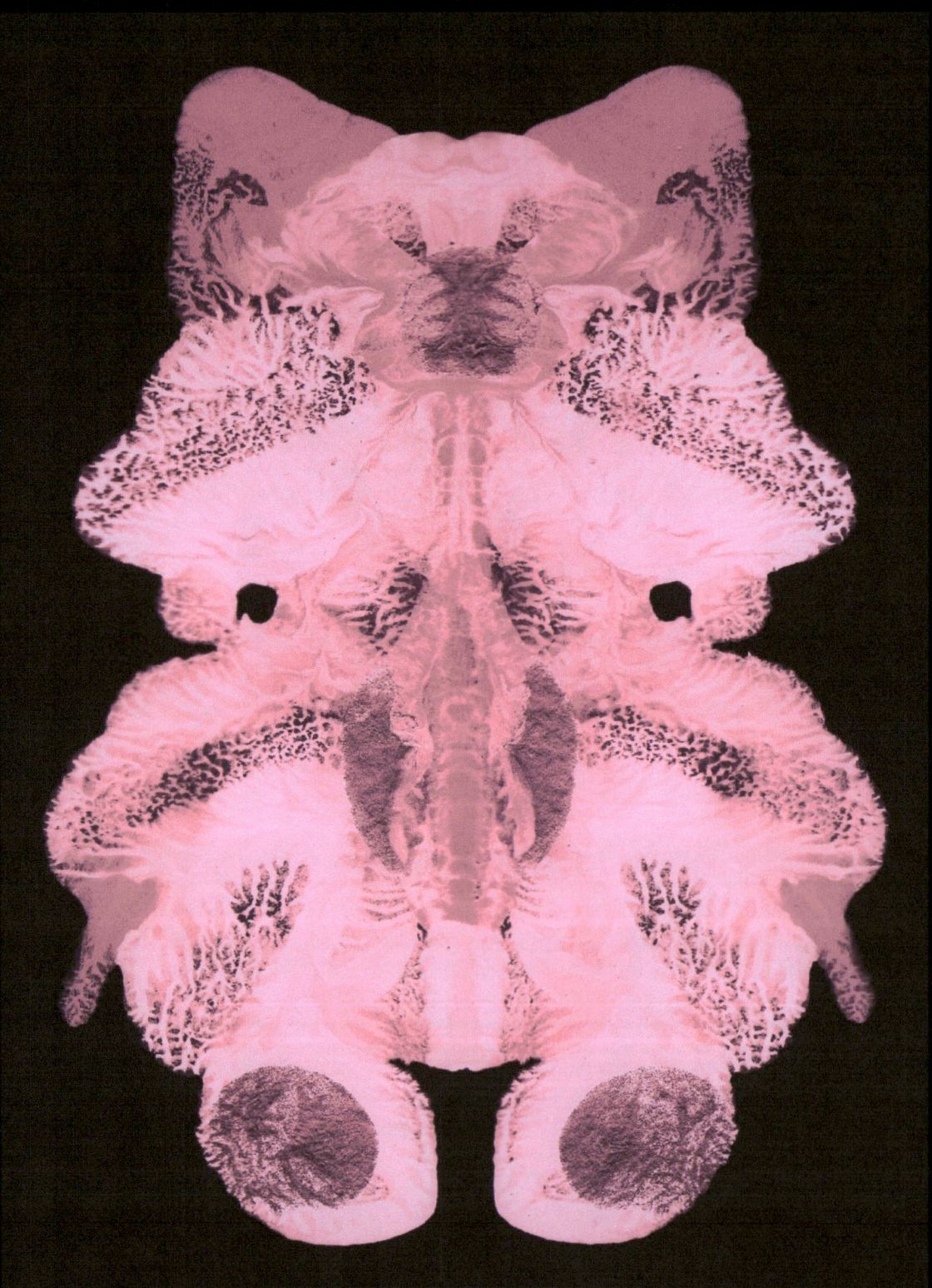

Image 136

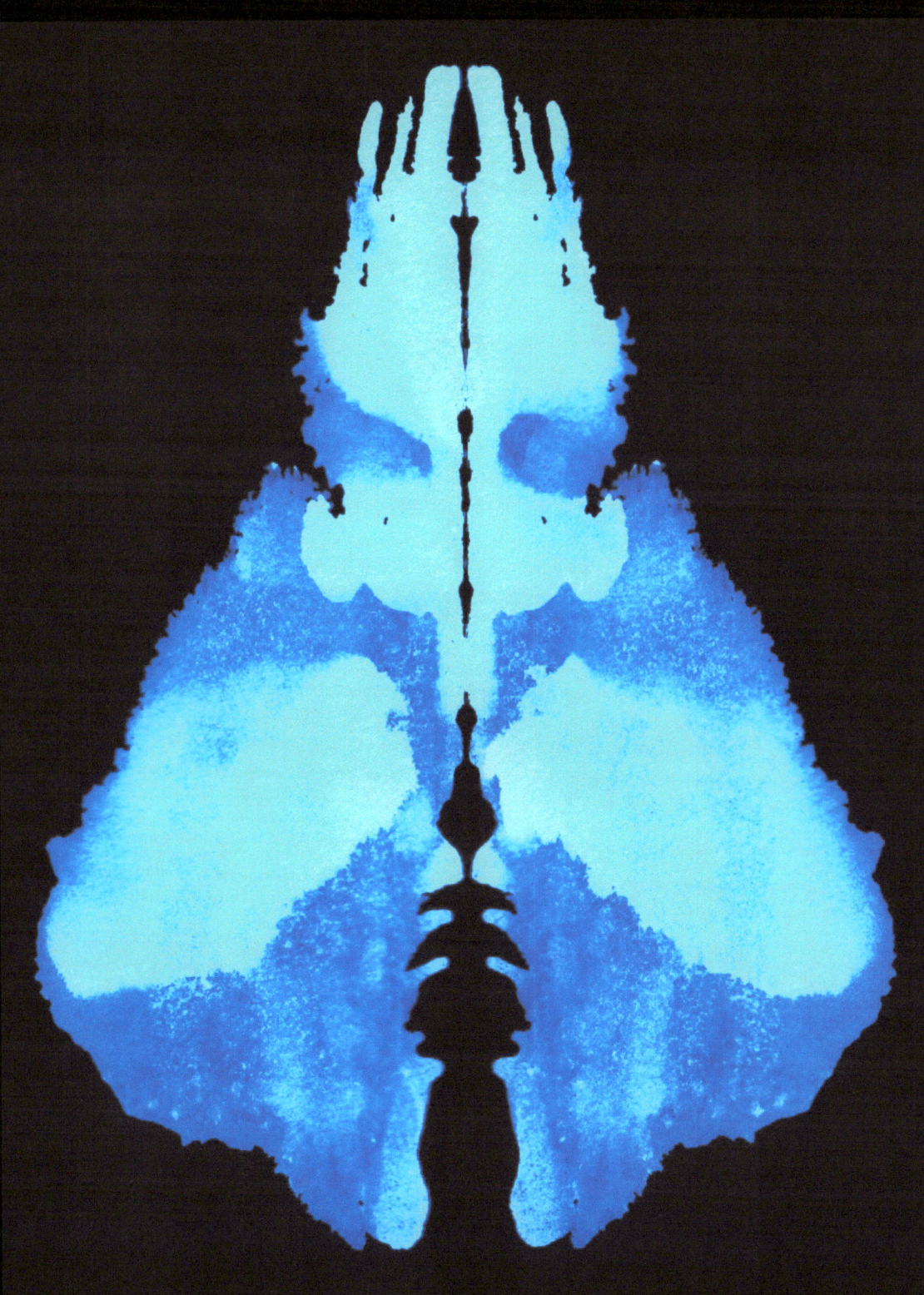

Image 137

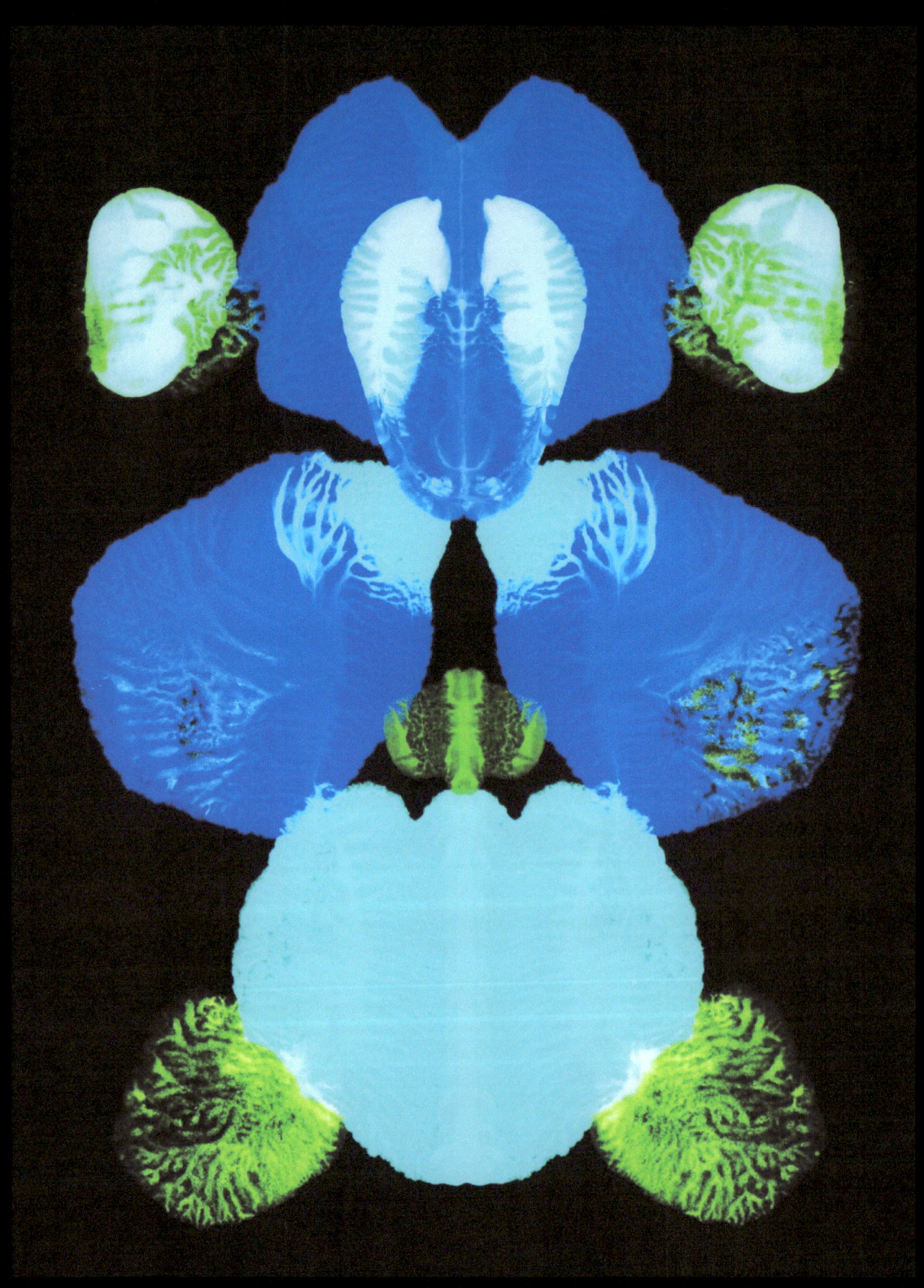

Image 138

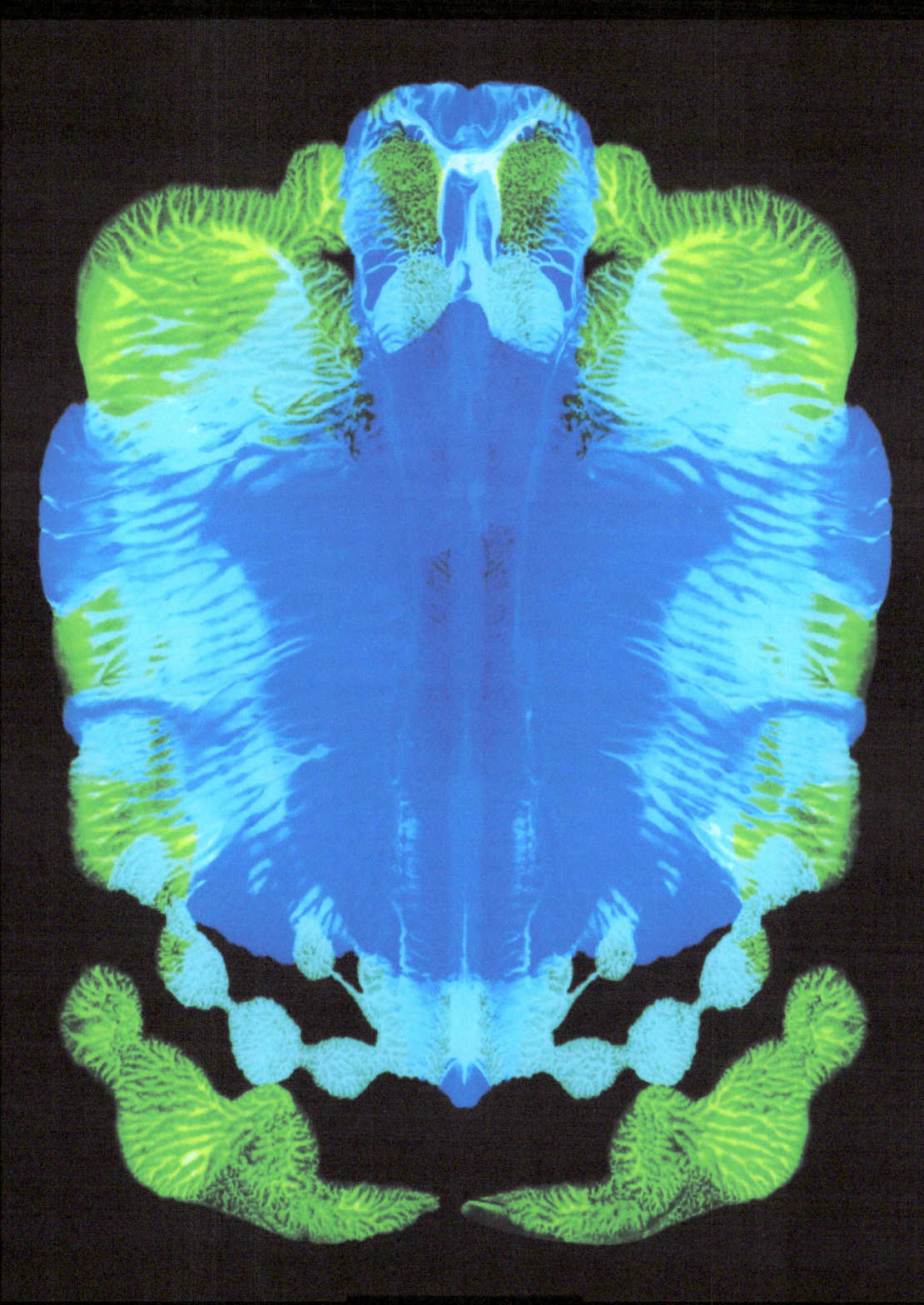

Image 139

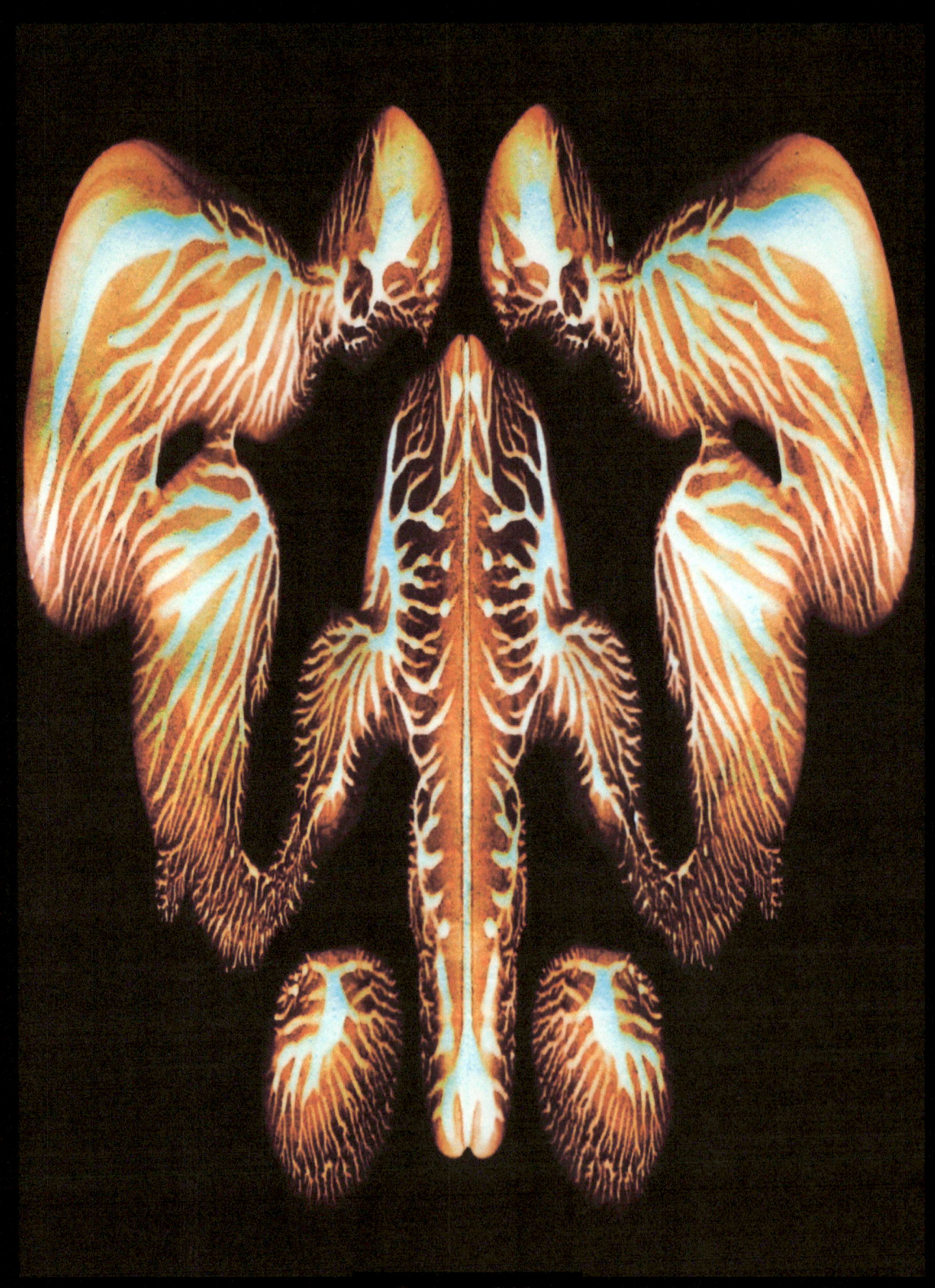

Image 140

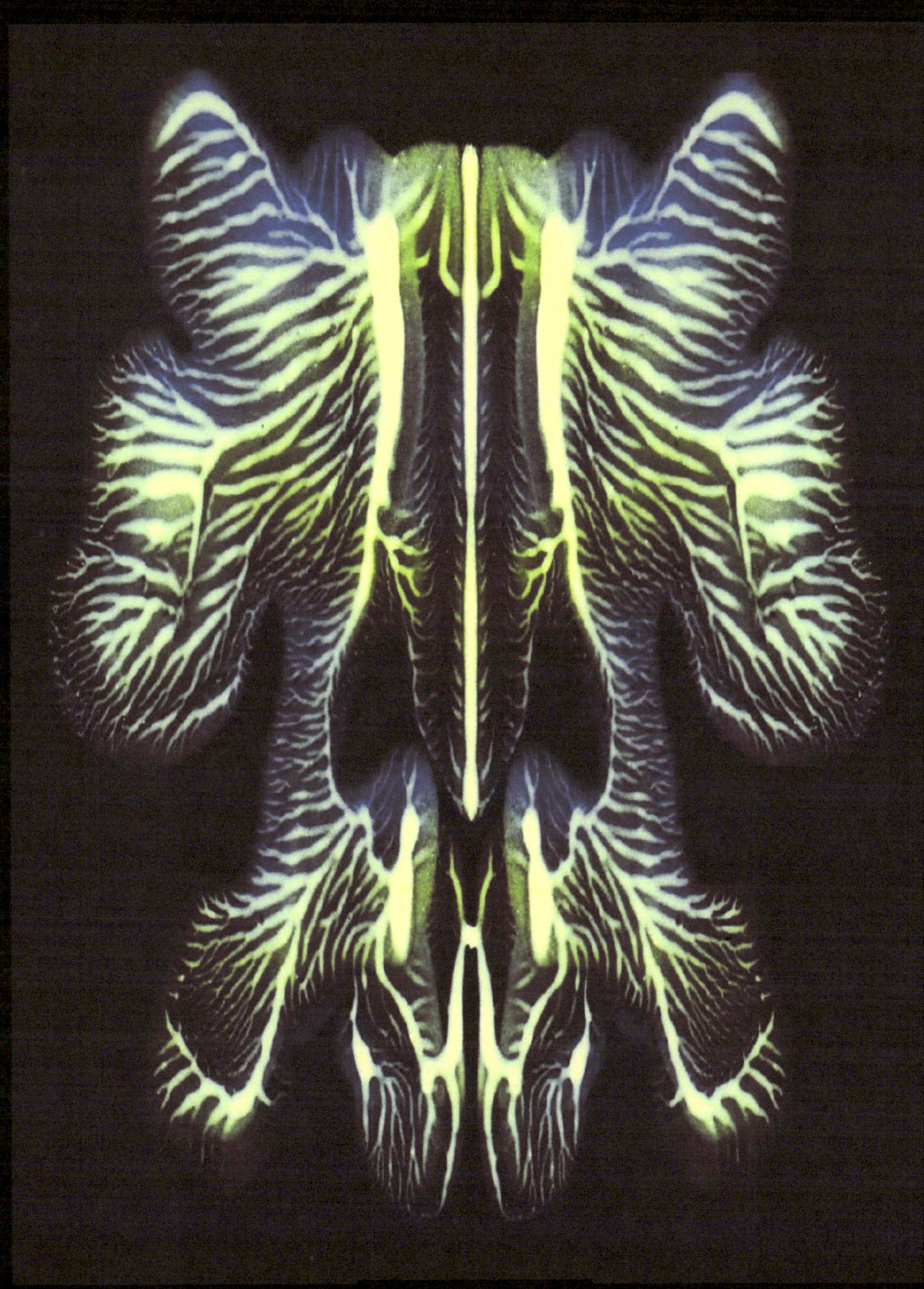

Image 141

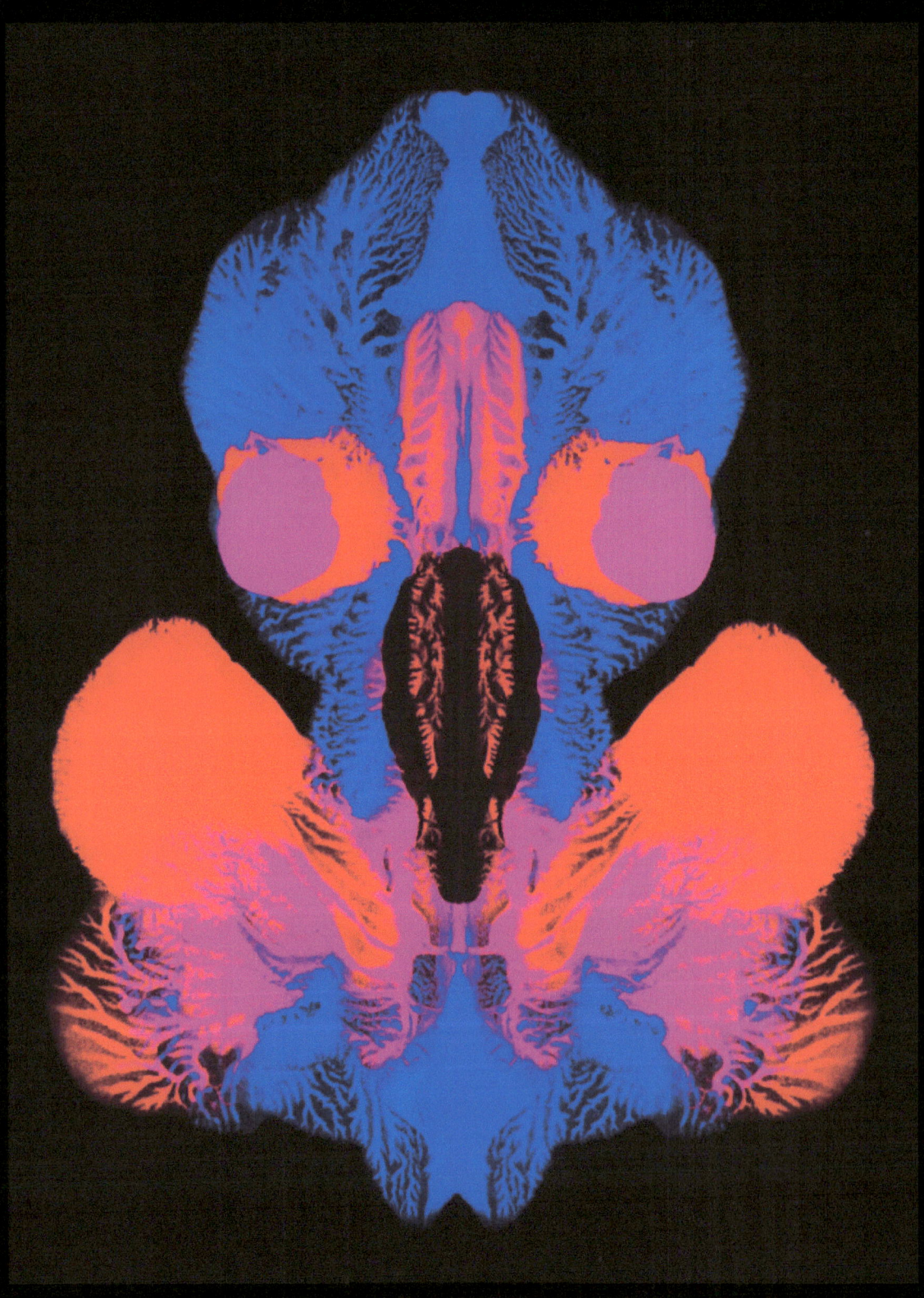

Image 142

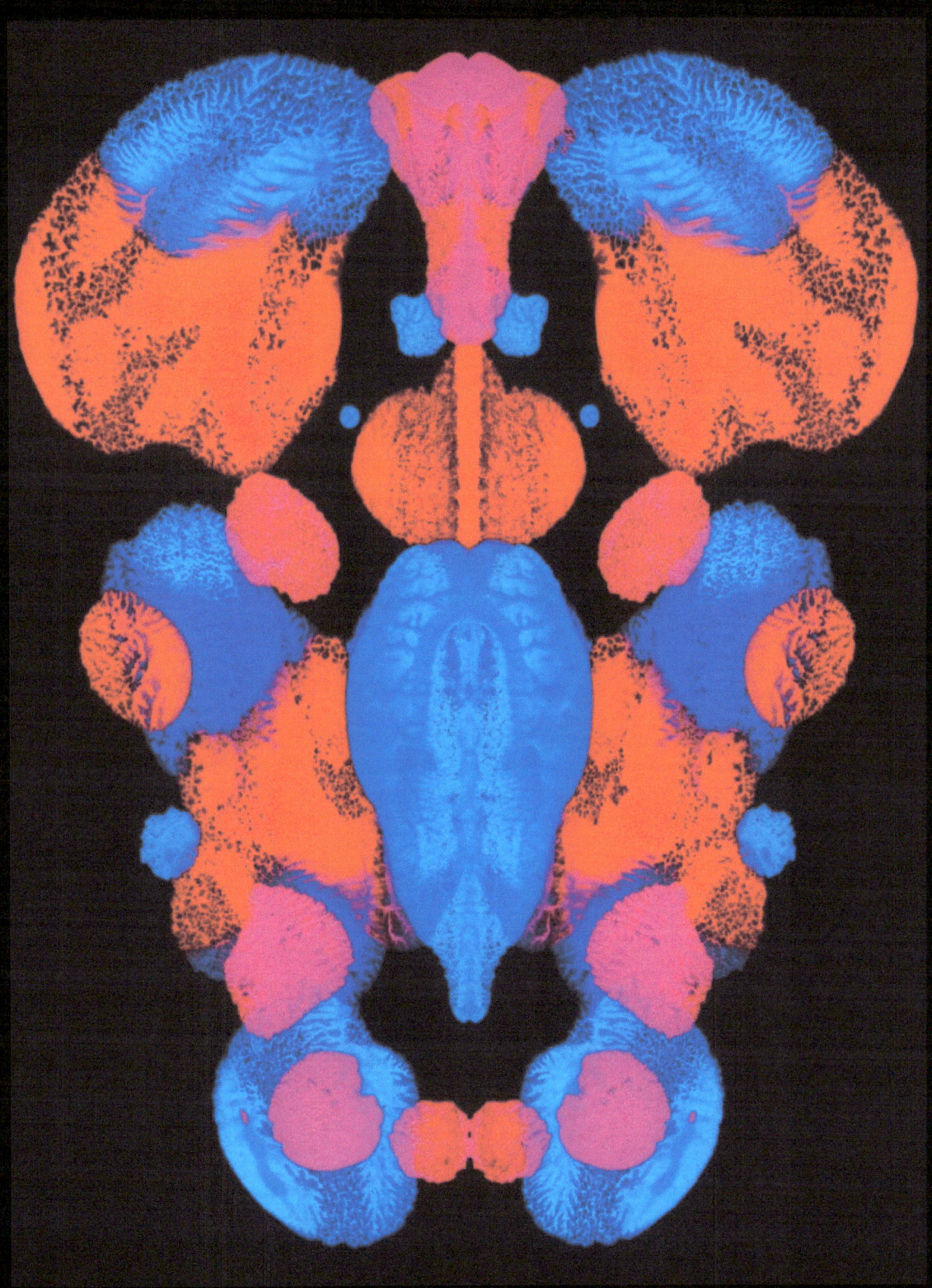

Image 143

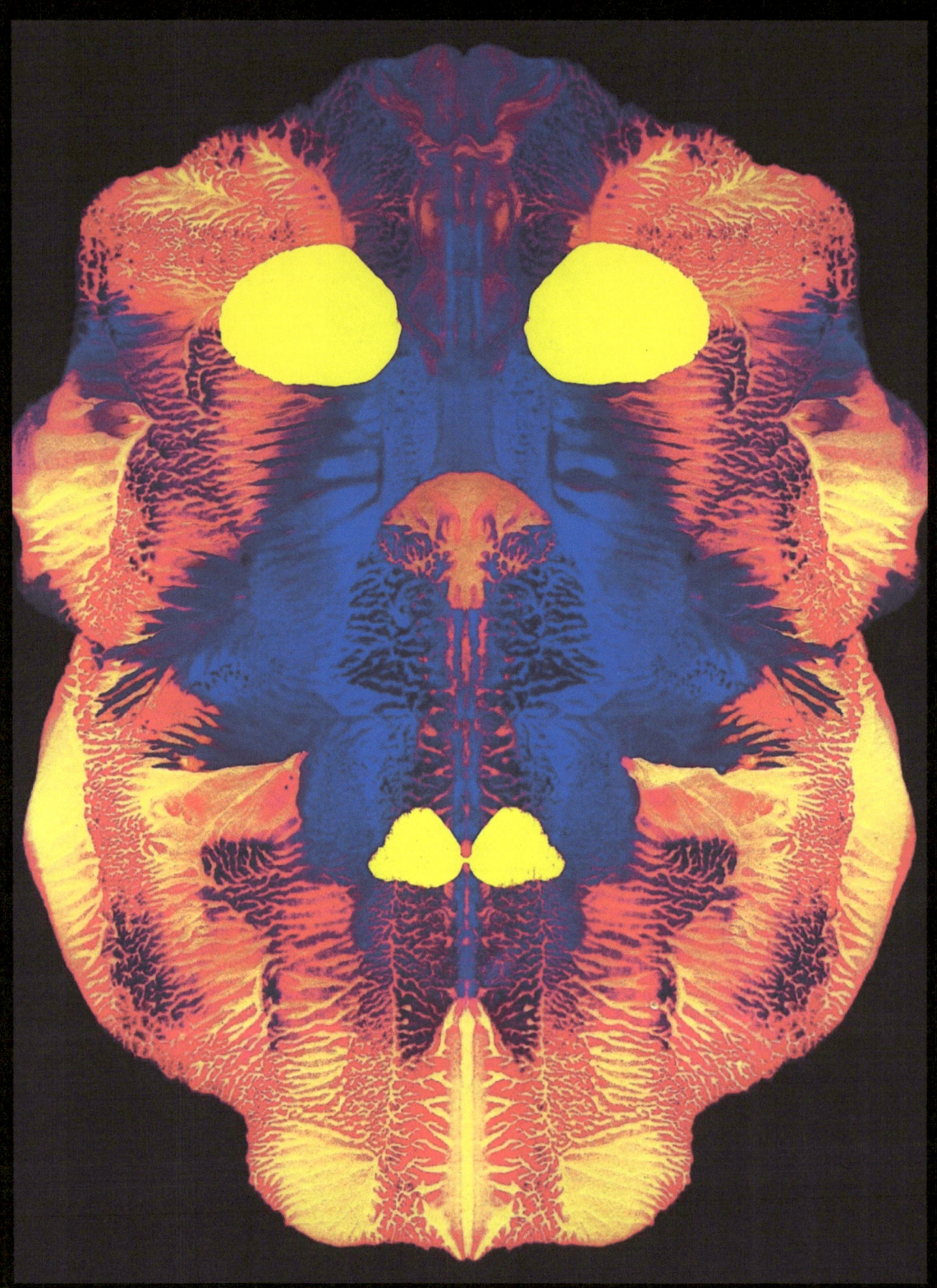

Image 144

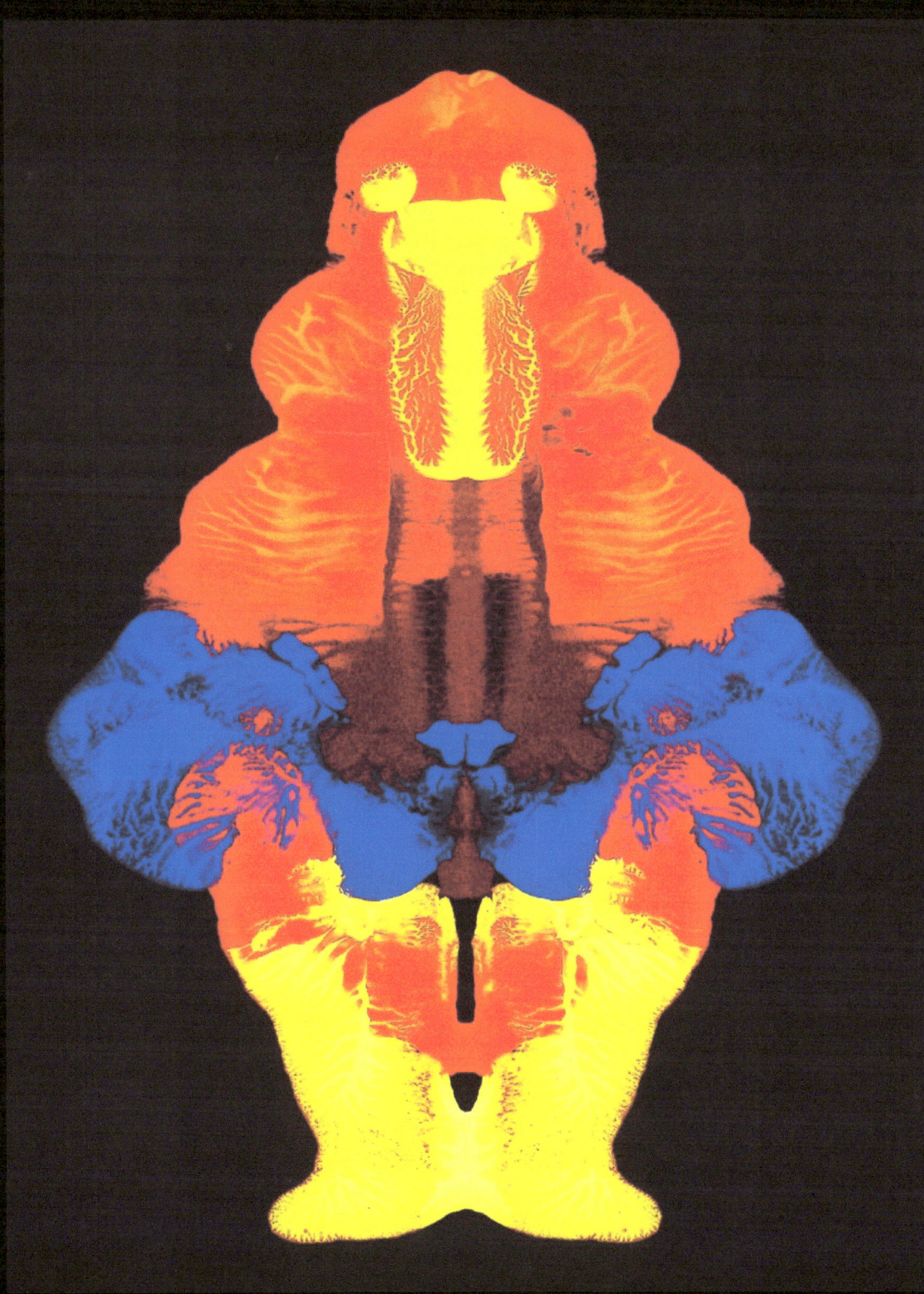

Image 145

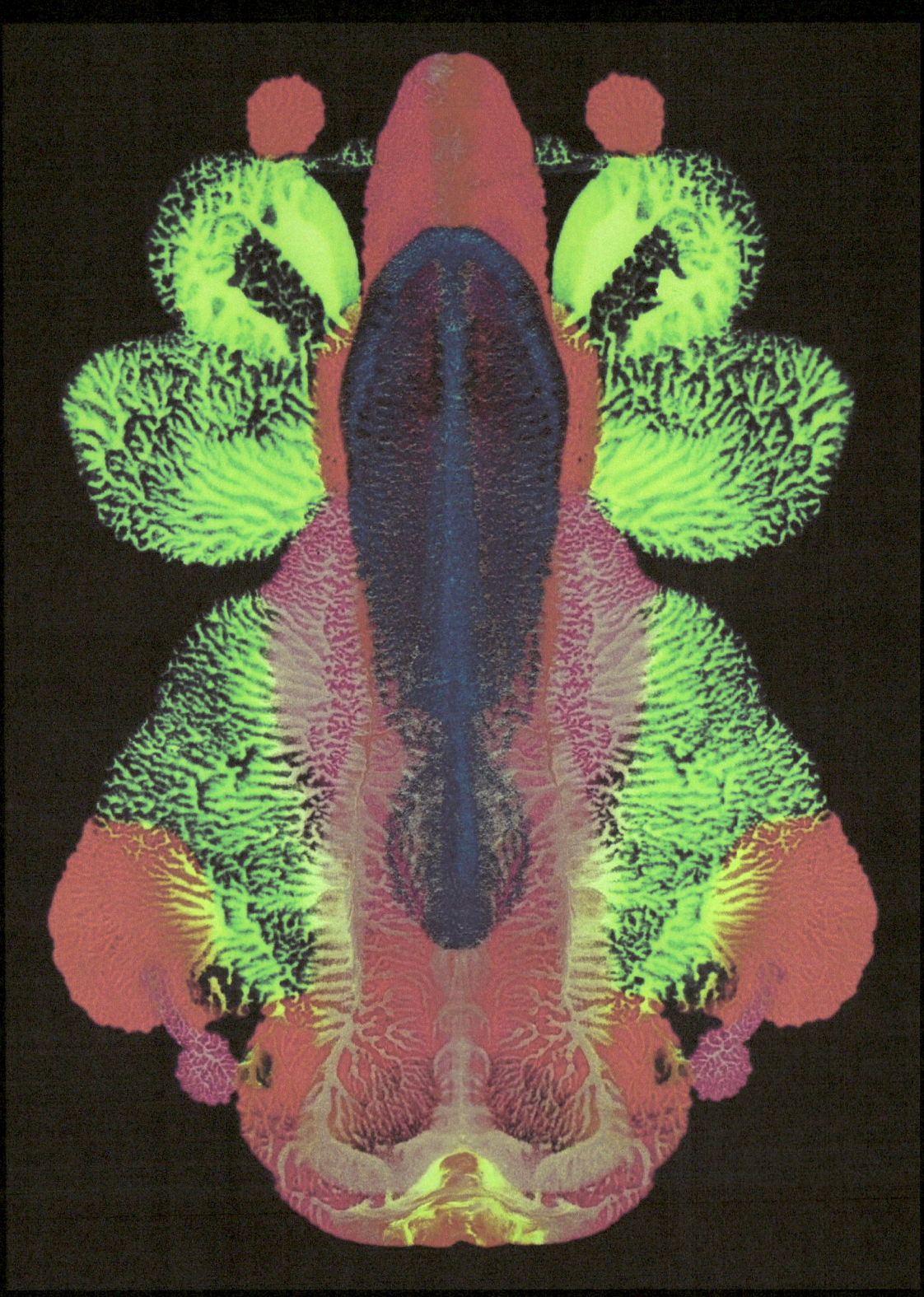

Image 146

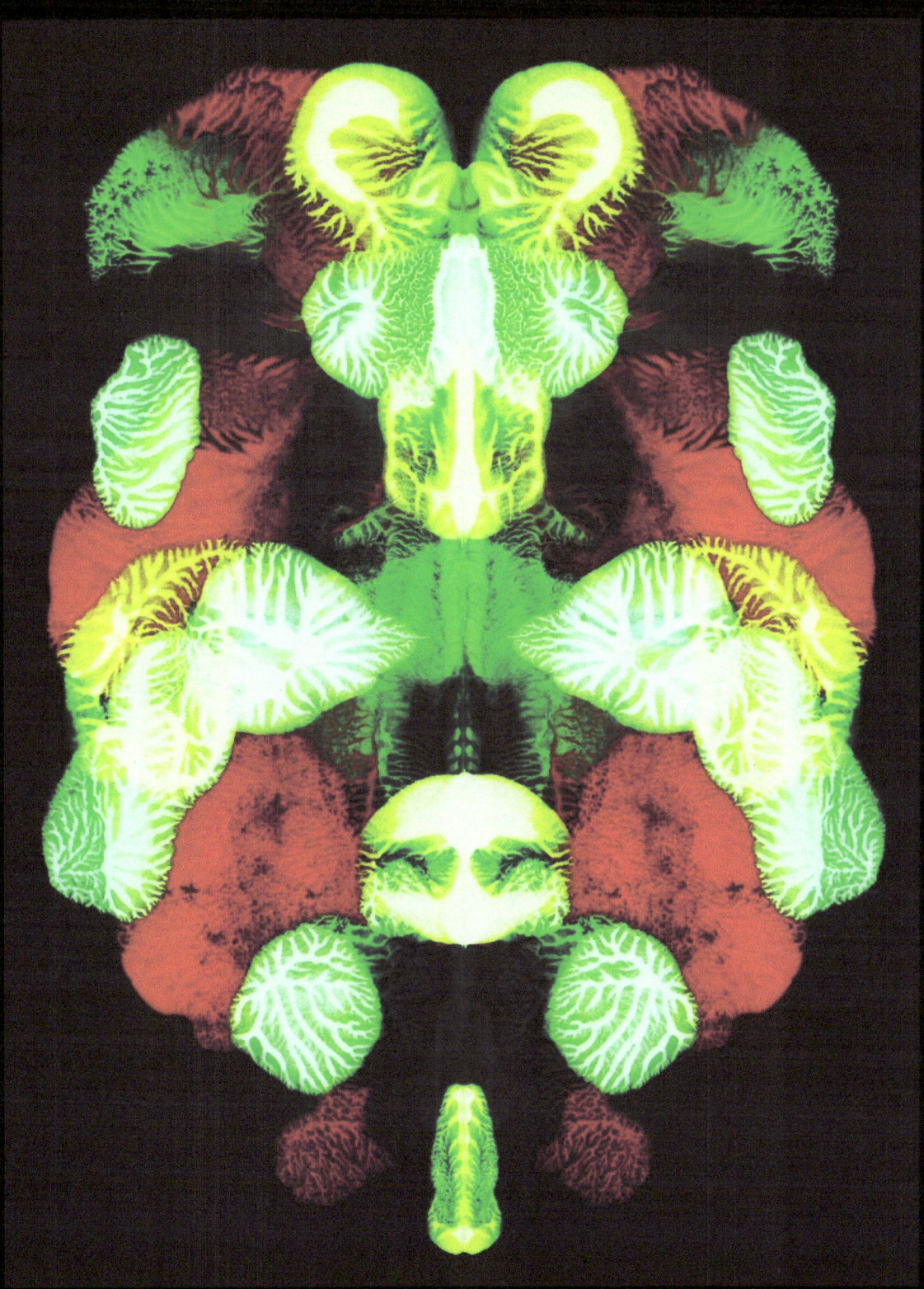

Image 147

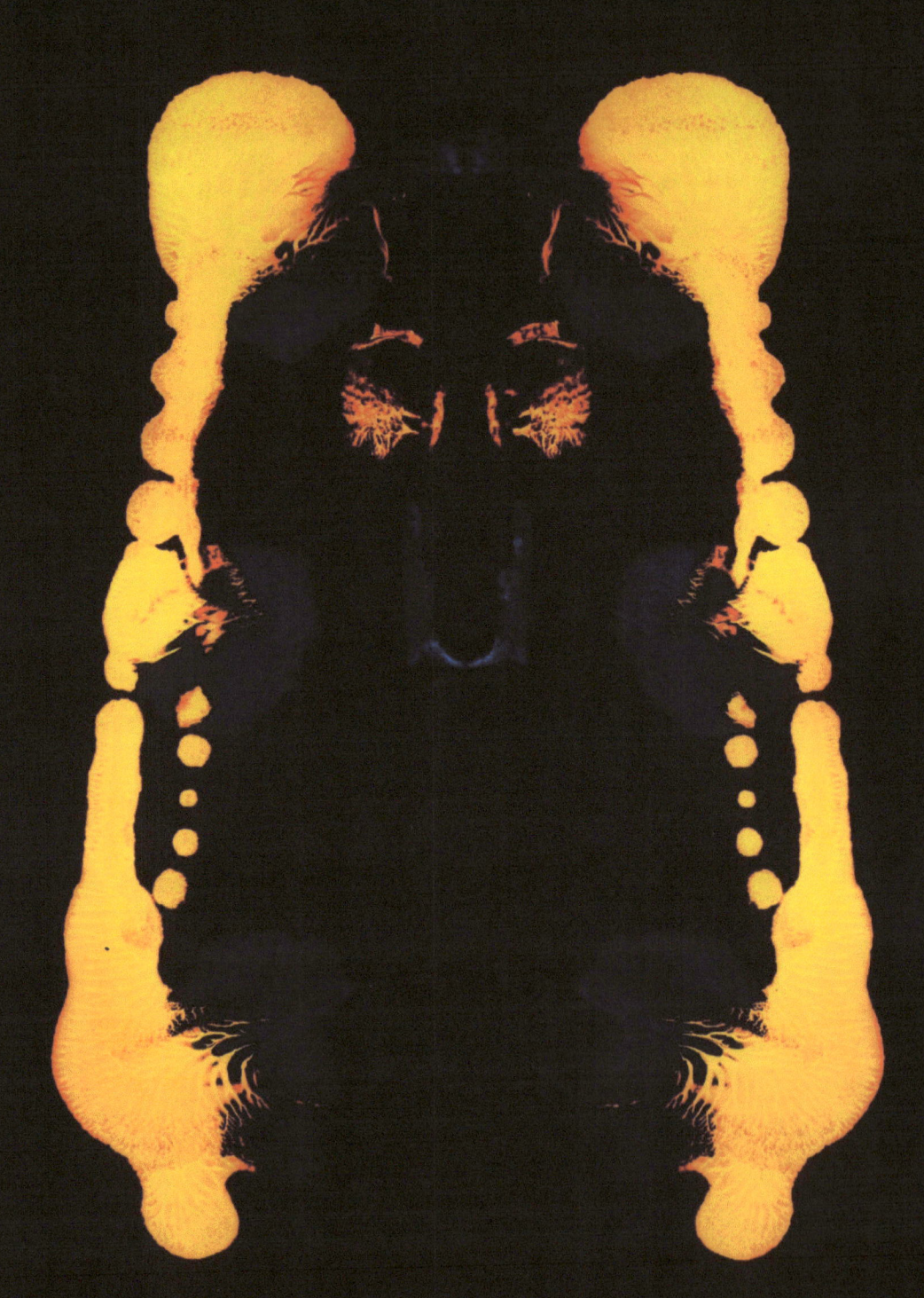
Image 148

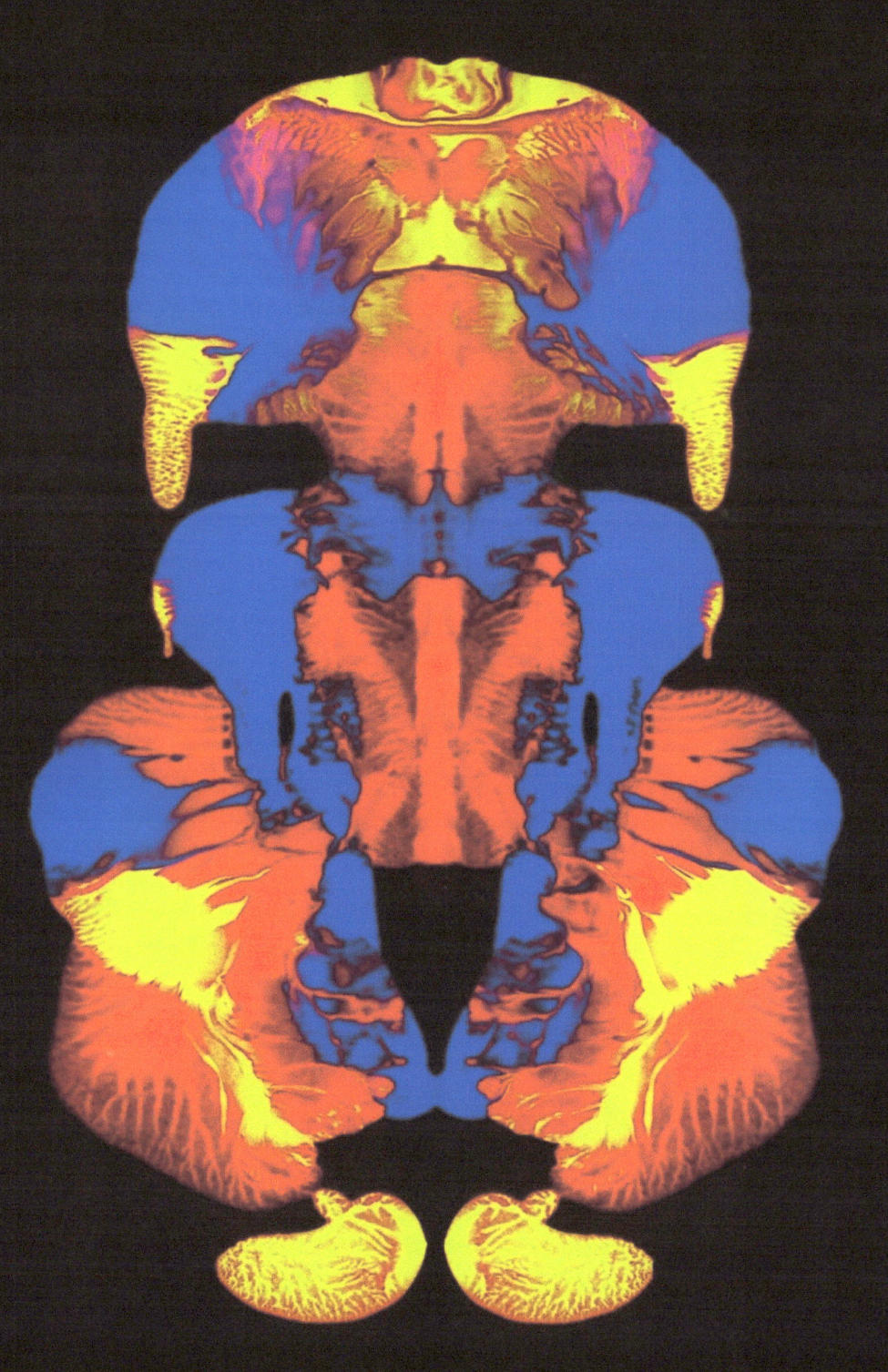

Image 149

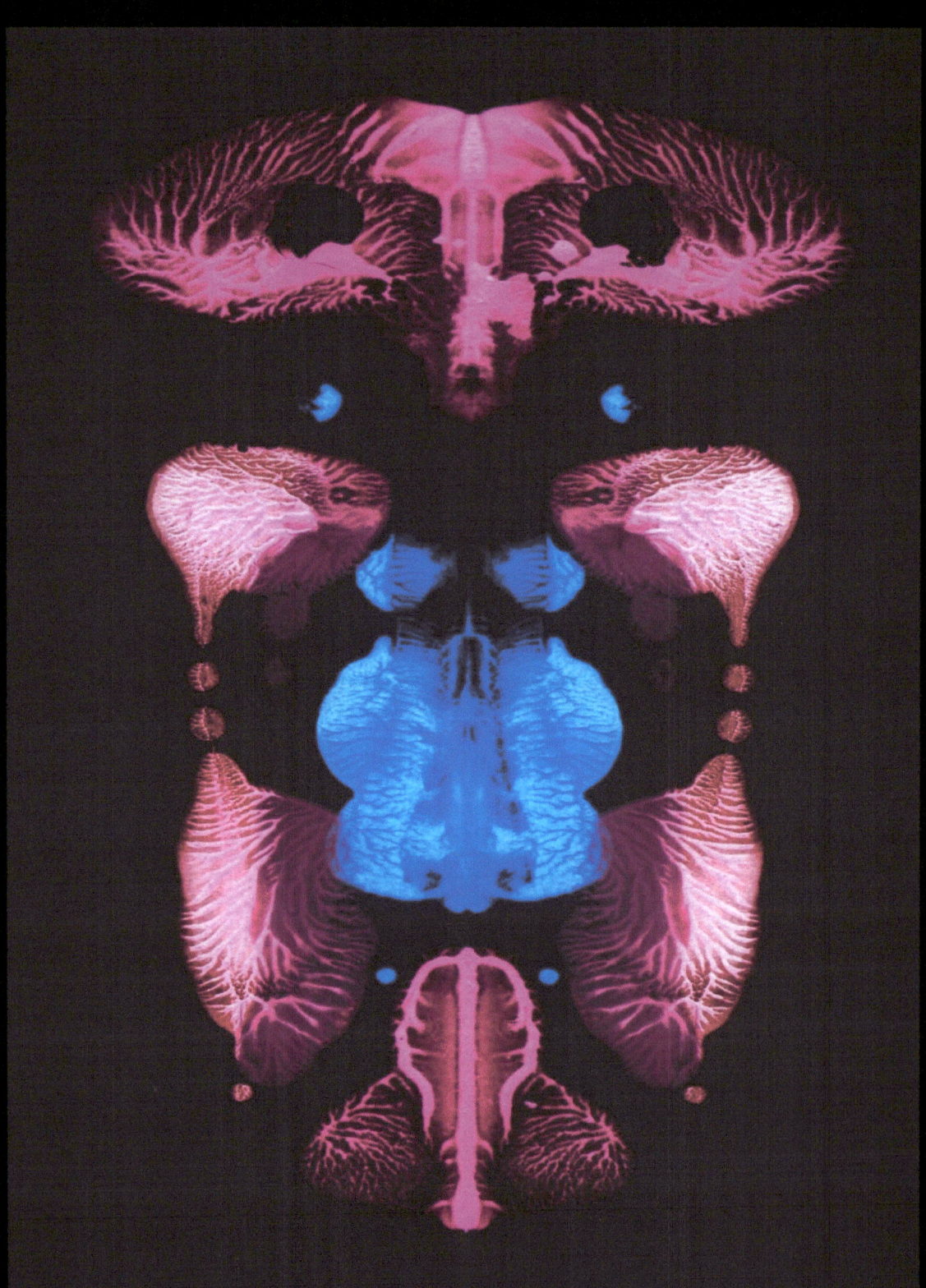

Image 150

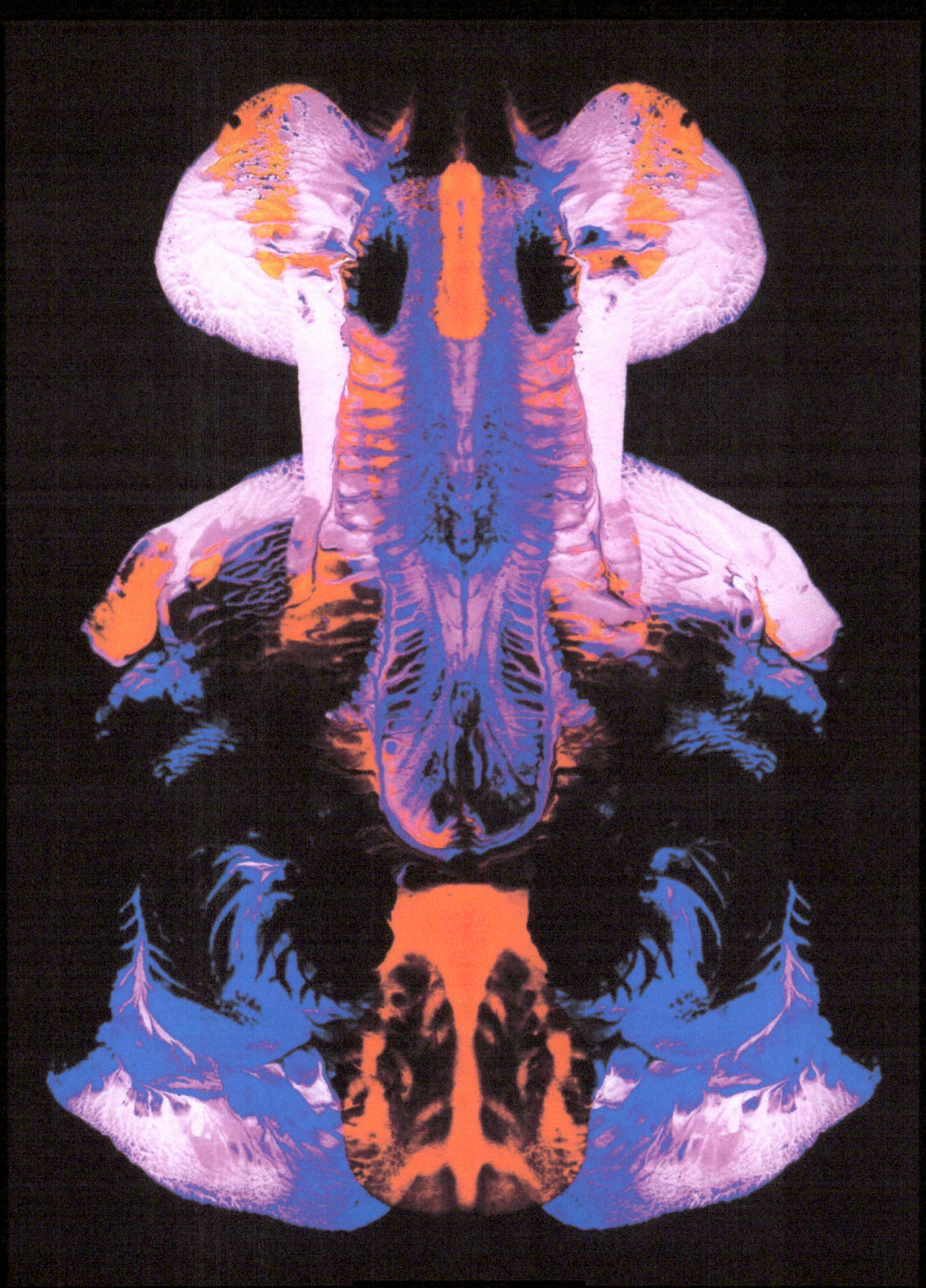

Image 151

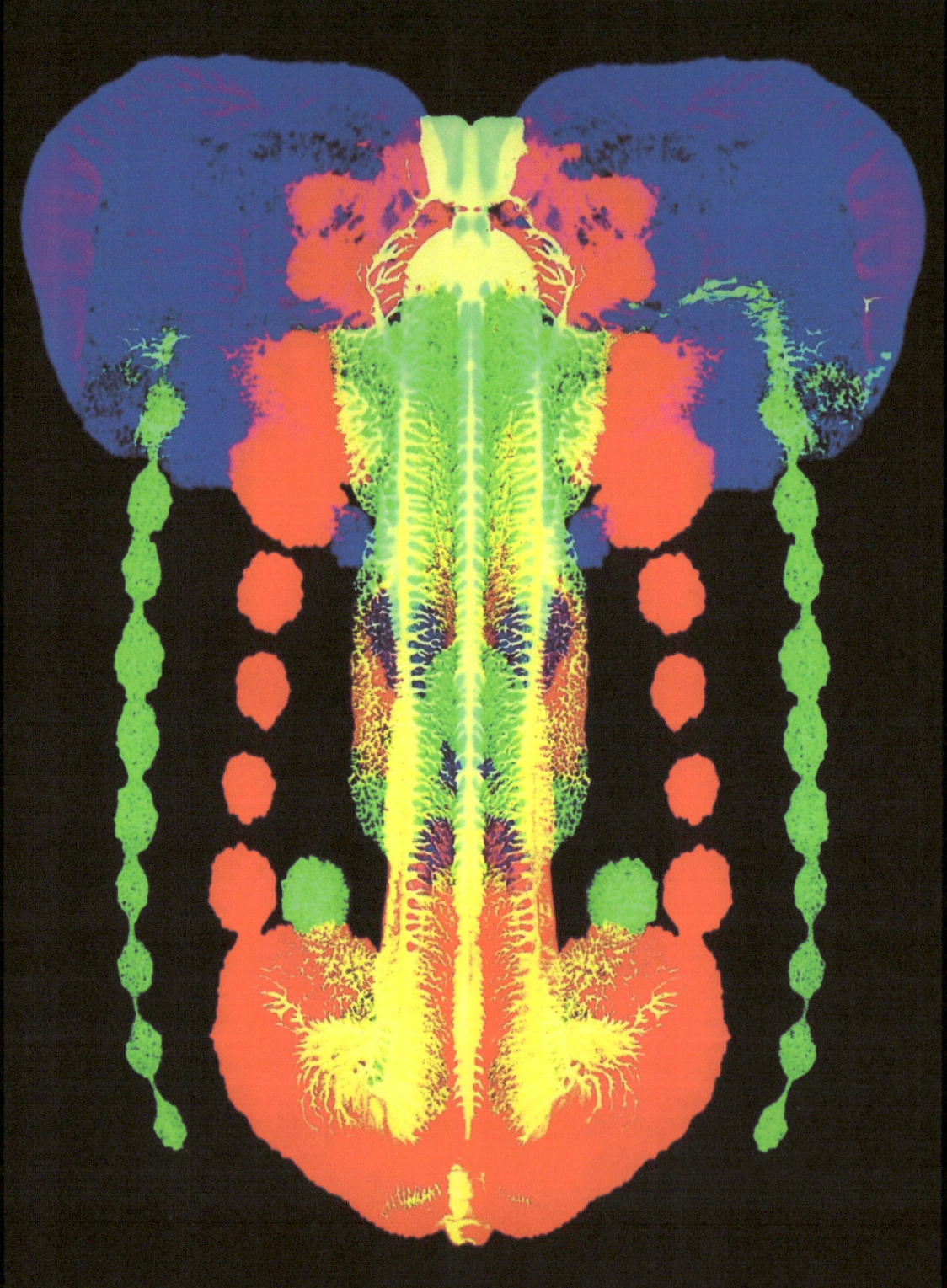

Image 152

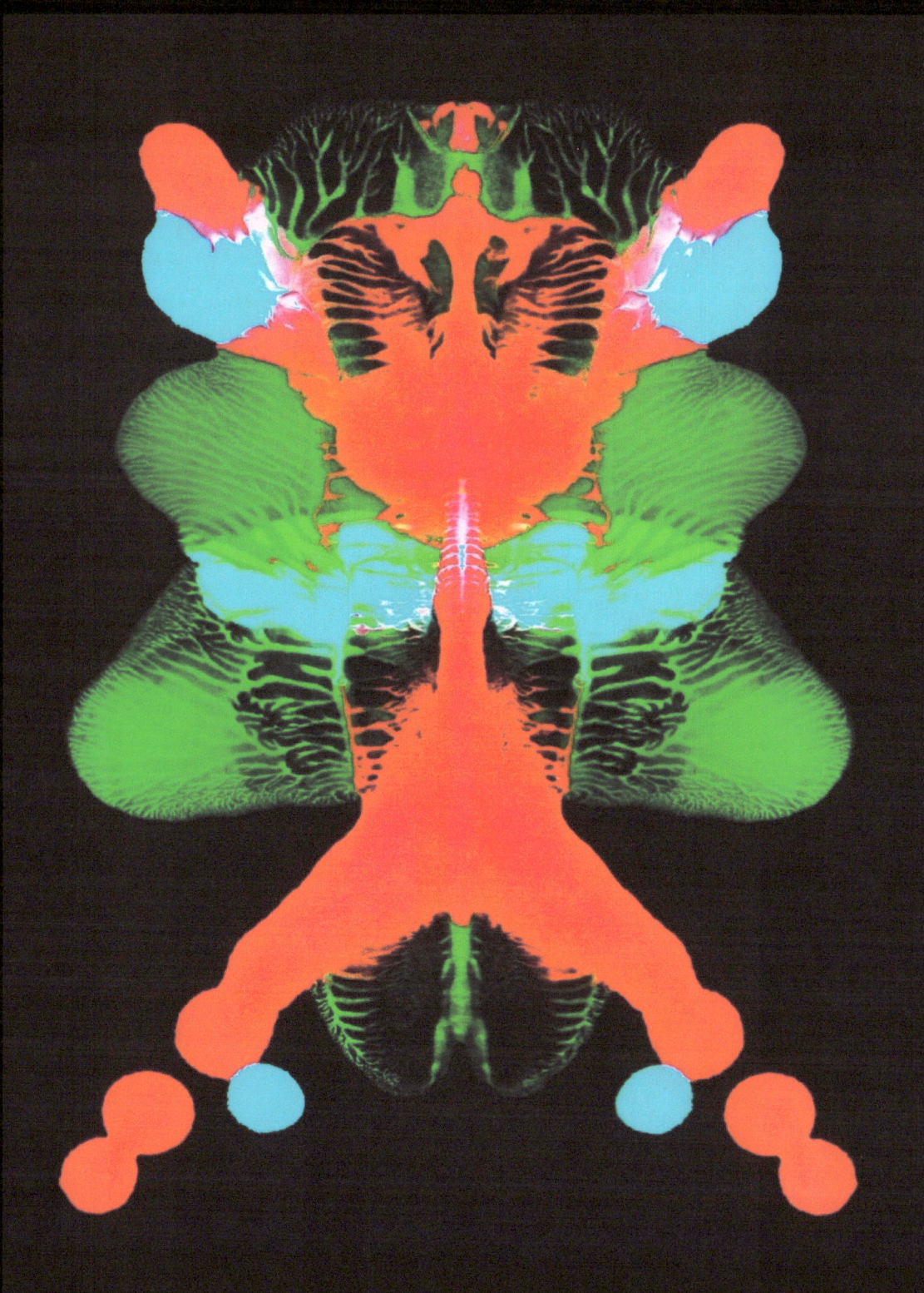

Image 153

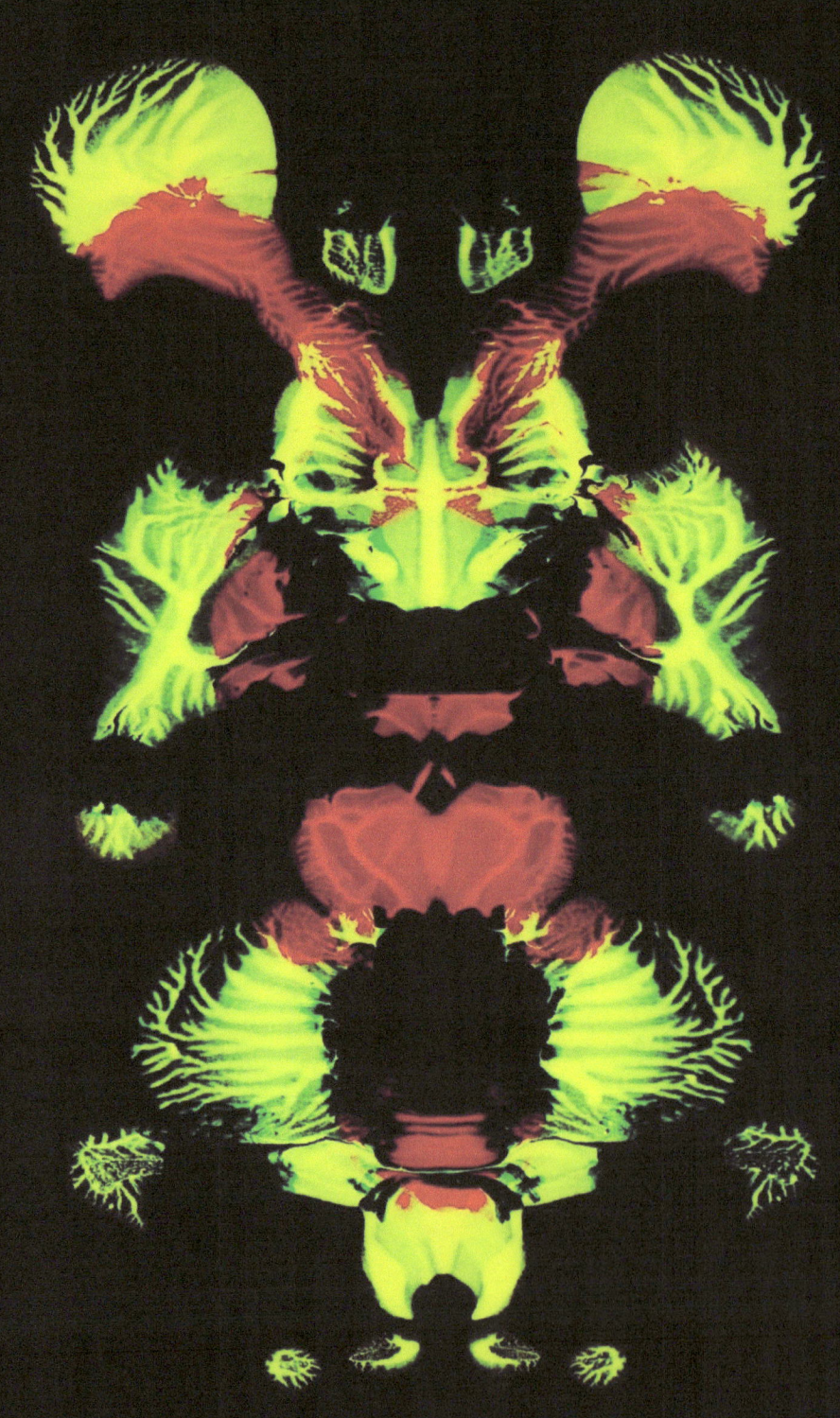

Image 154

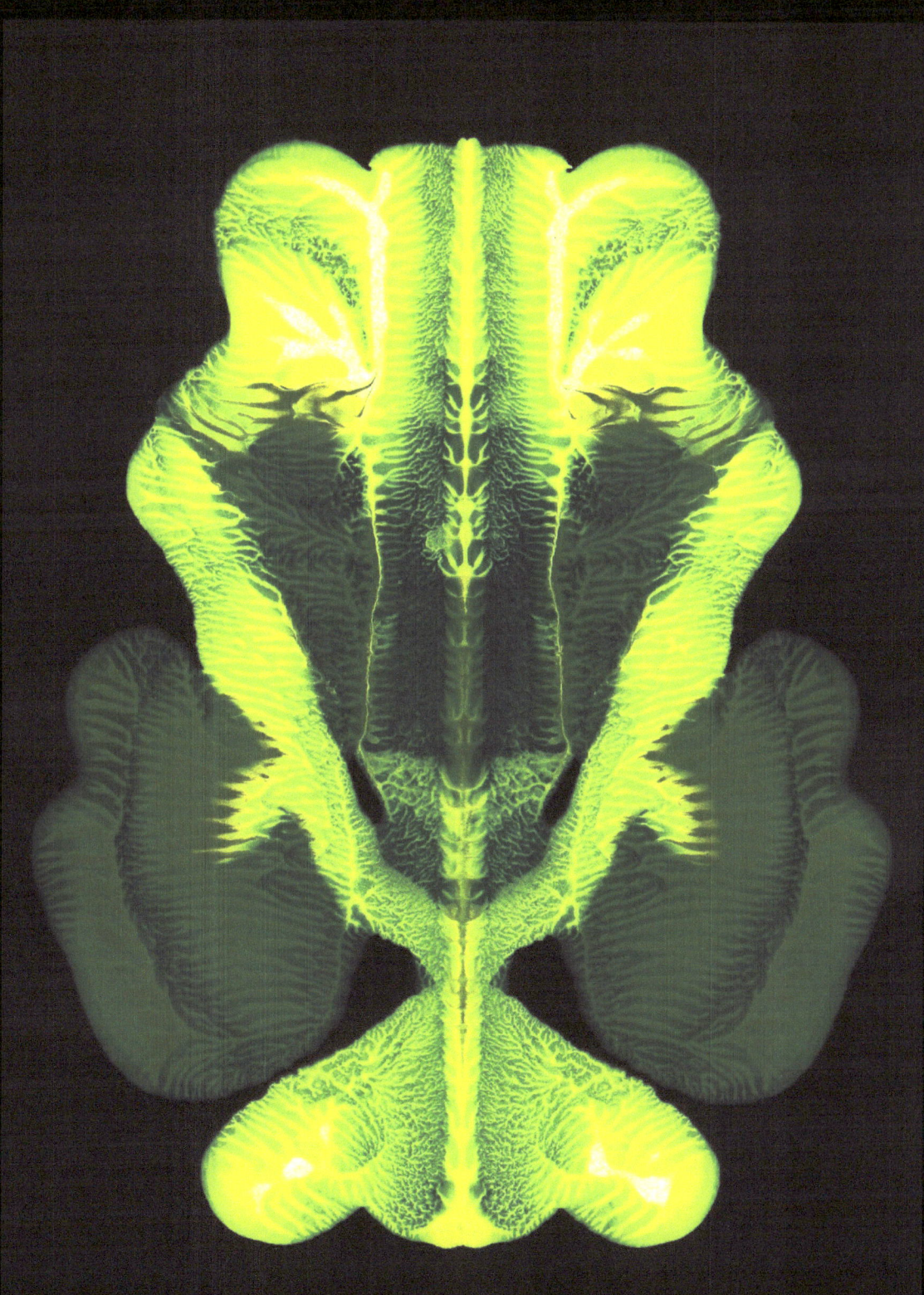

Image 155

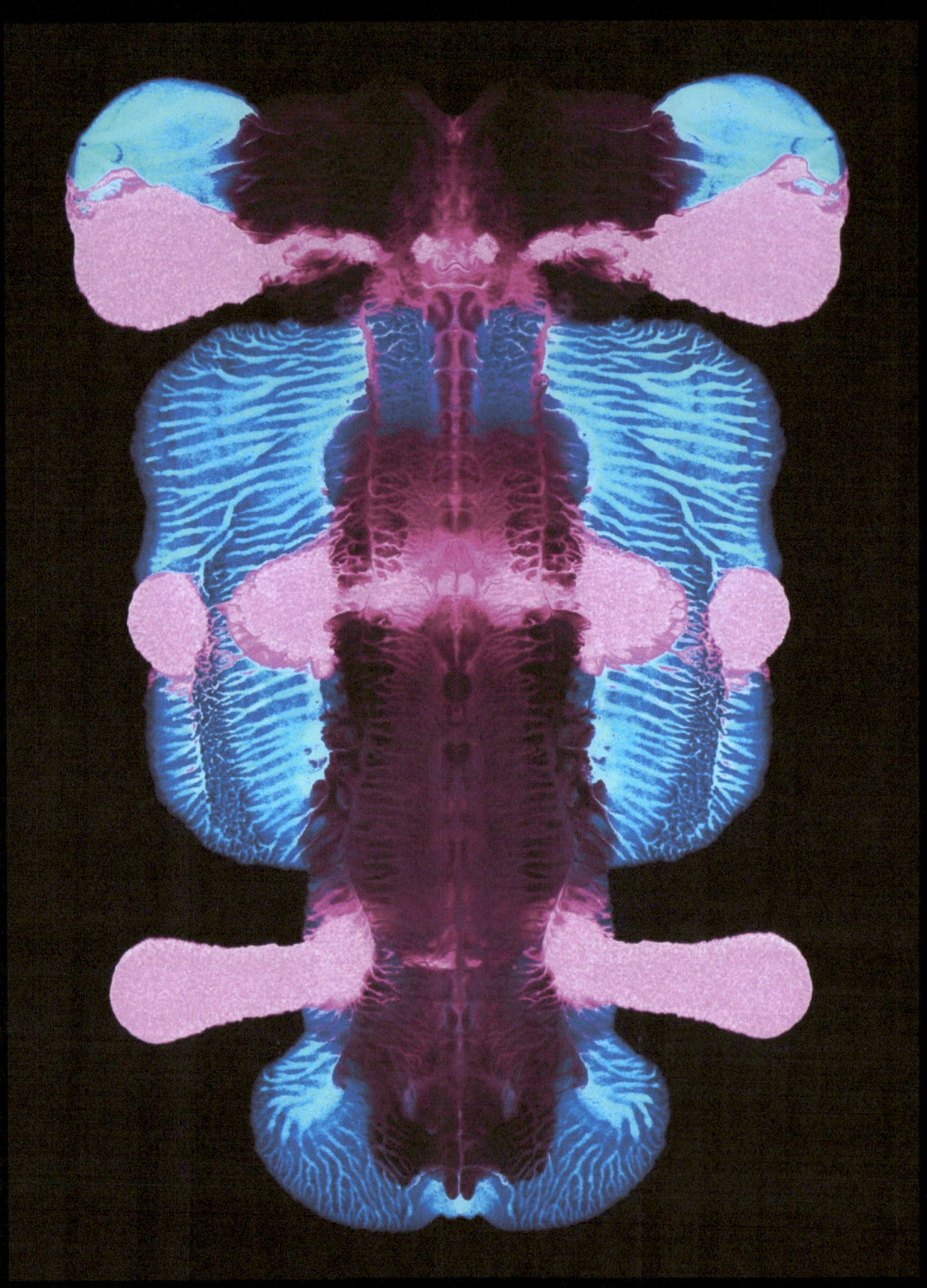

Image 156

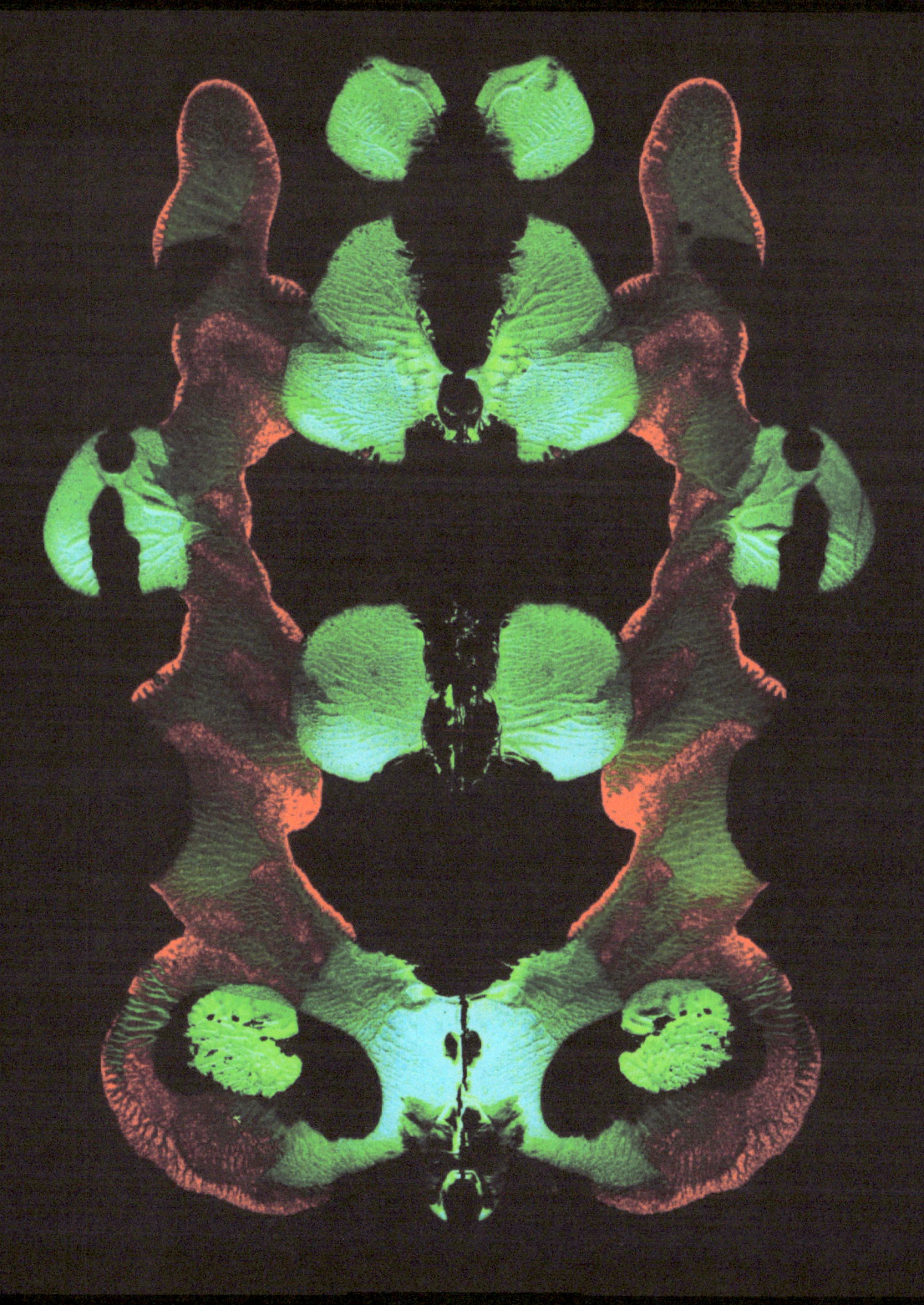

Image 157

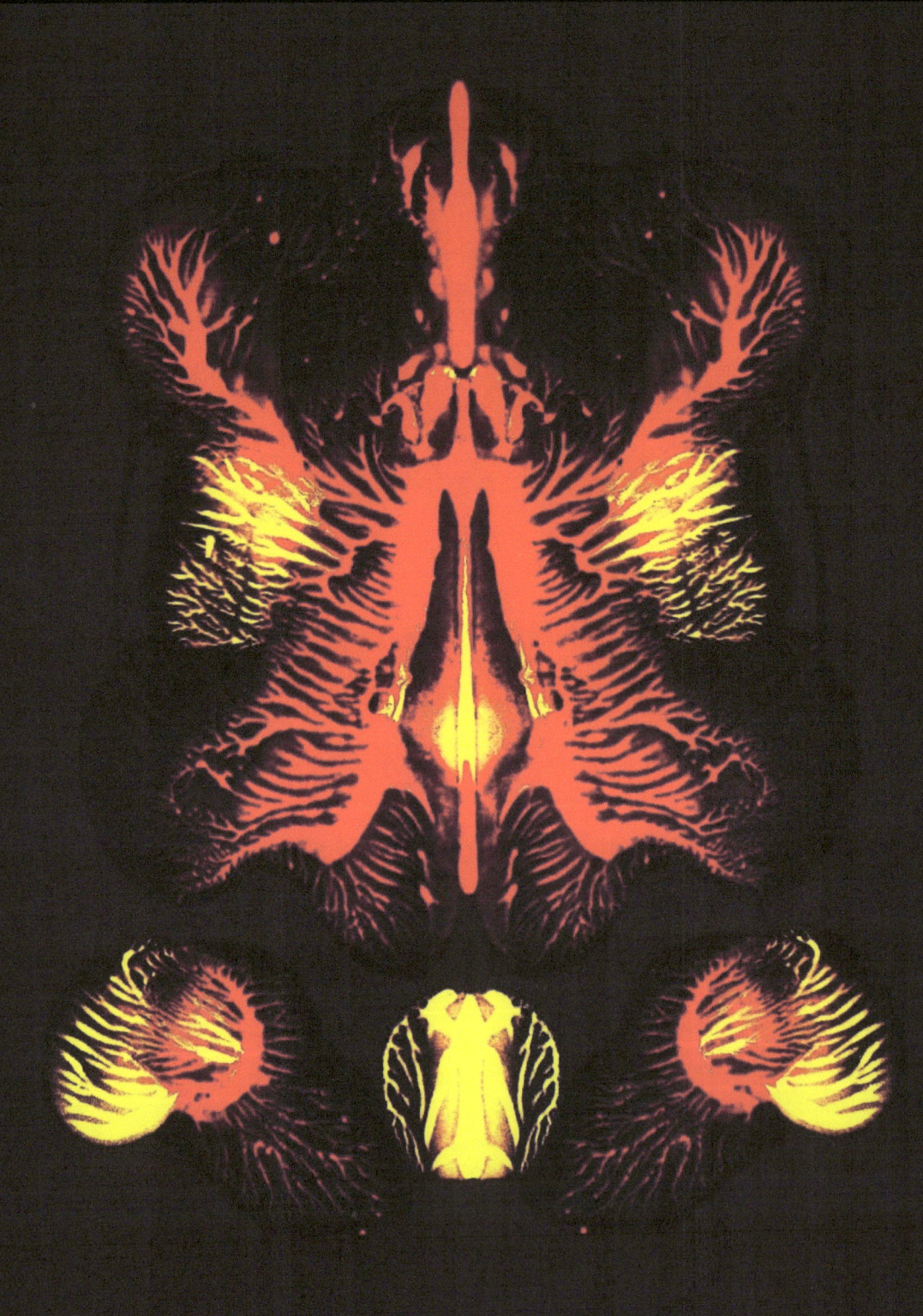

Image 158

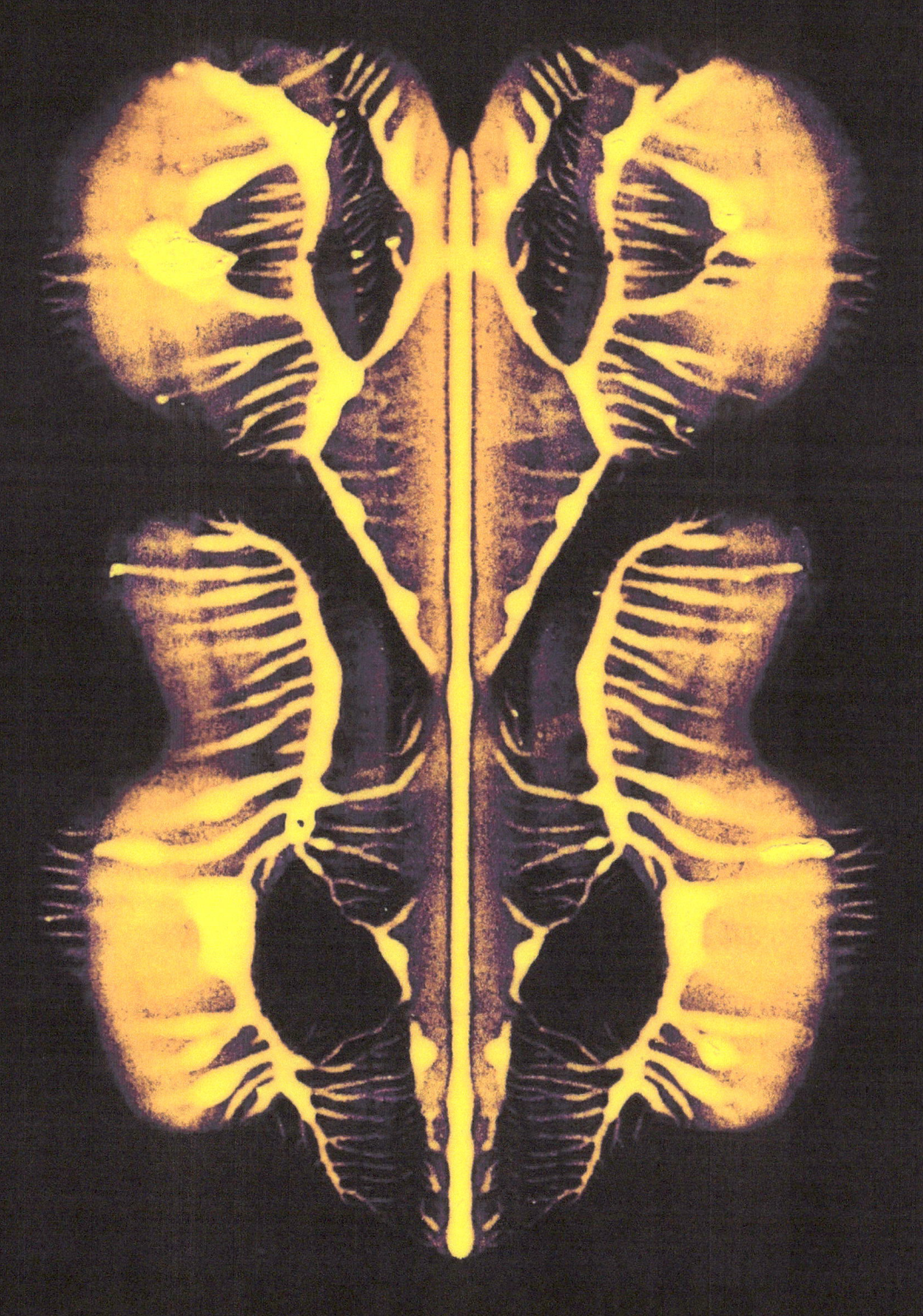

Image 159

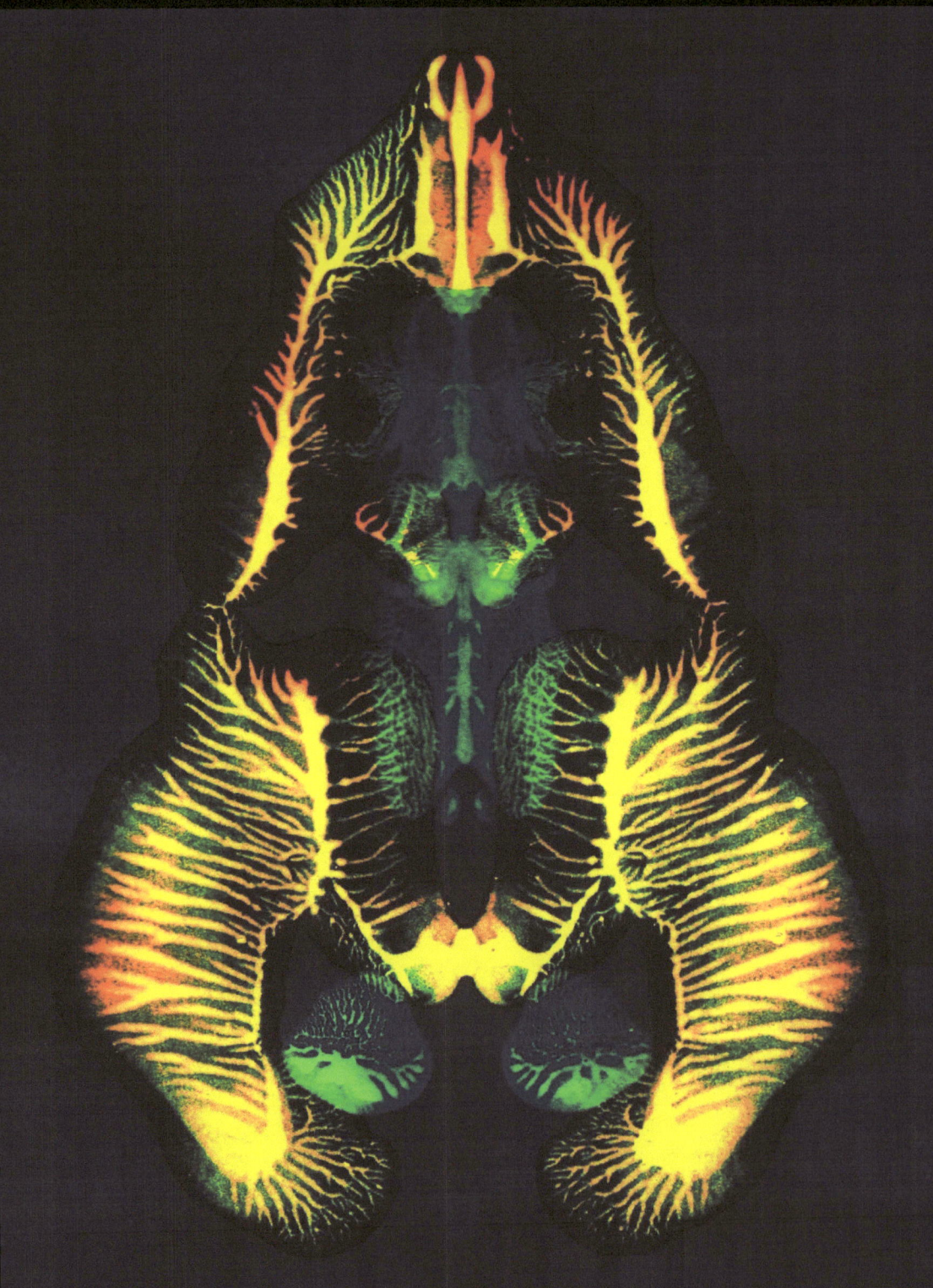

Image 160

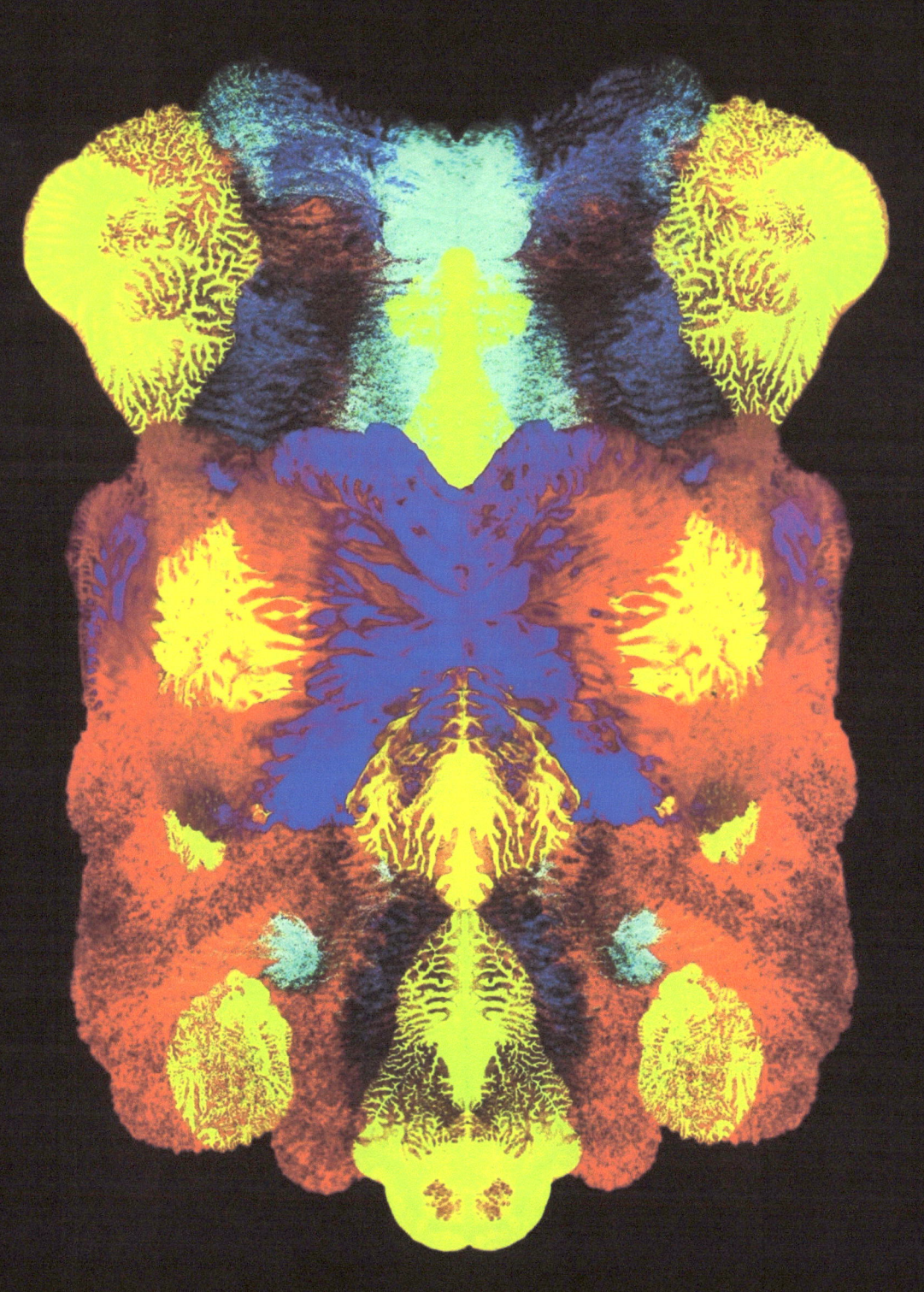

Image 161

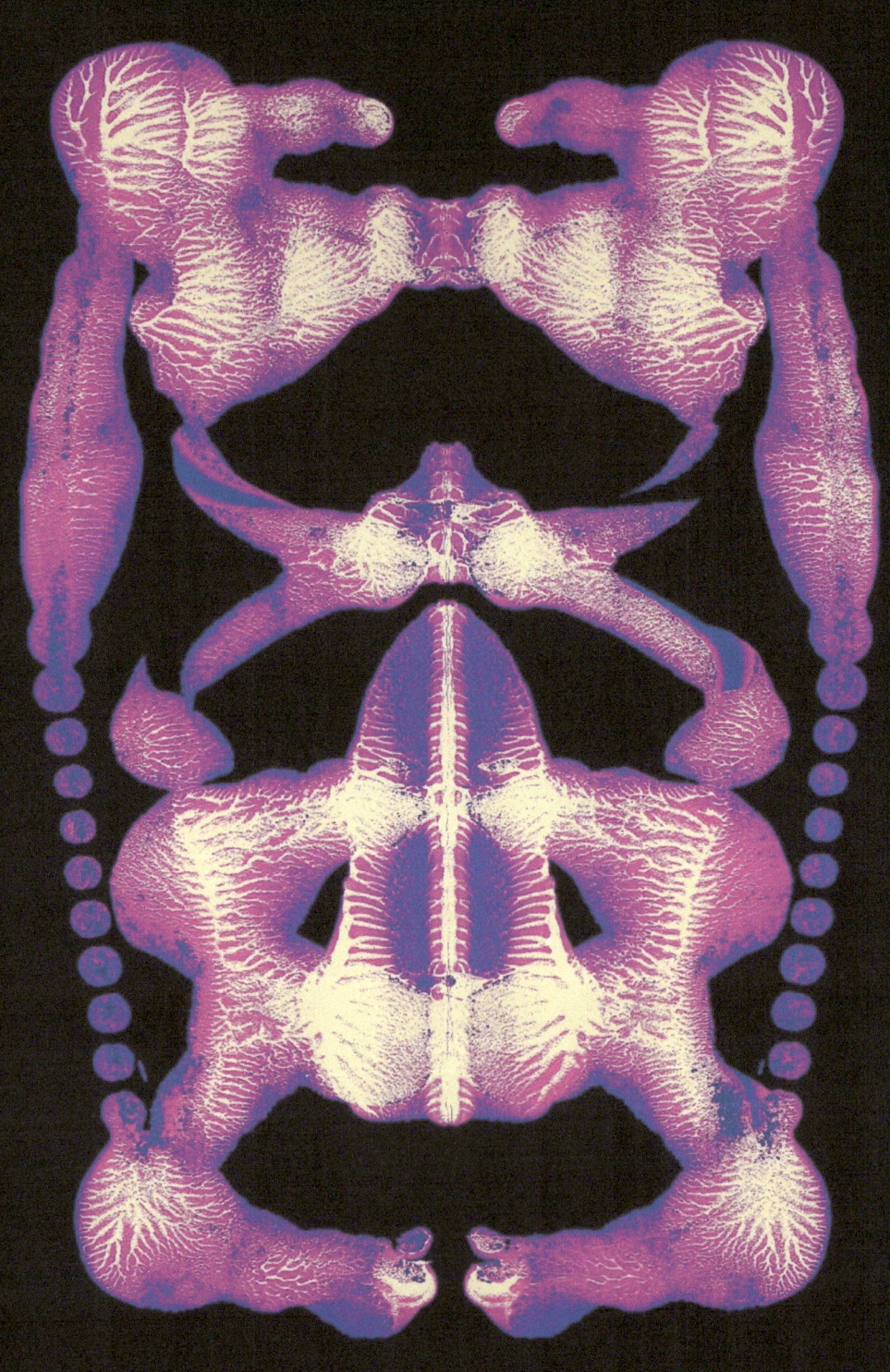

Image 162

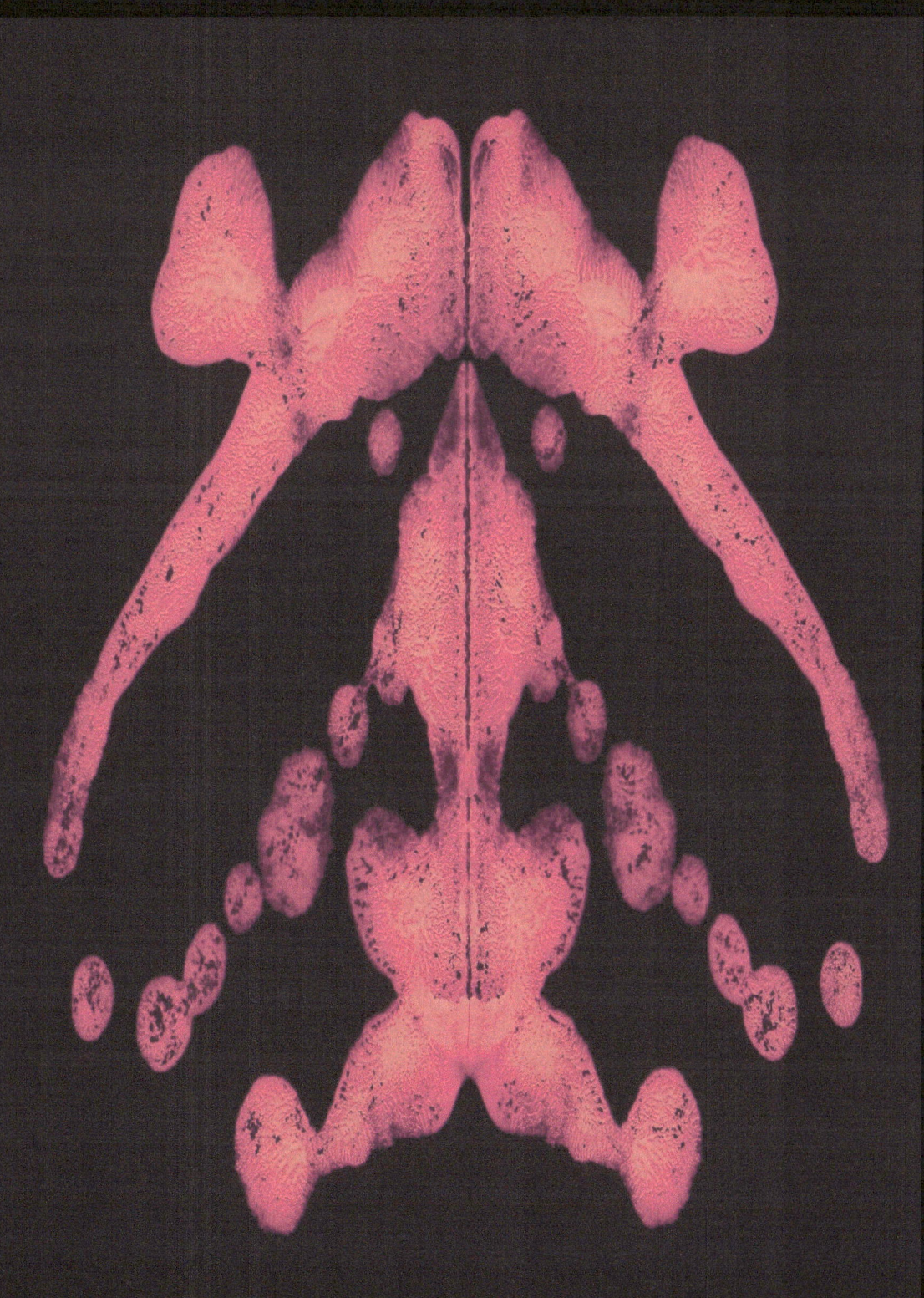

Image 163

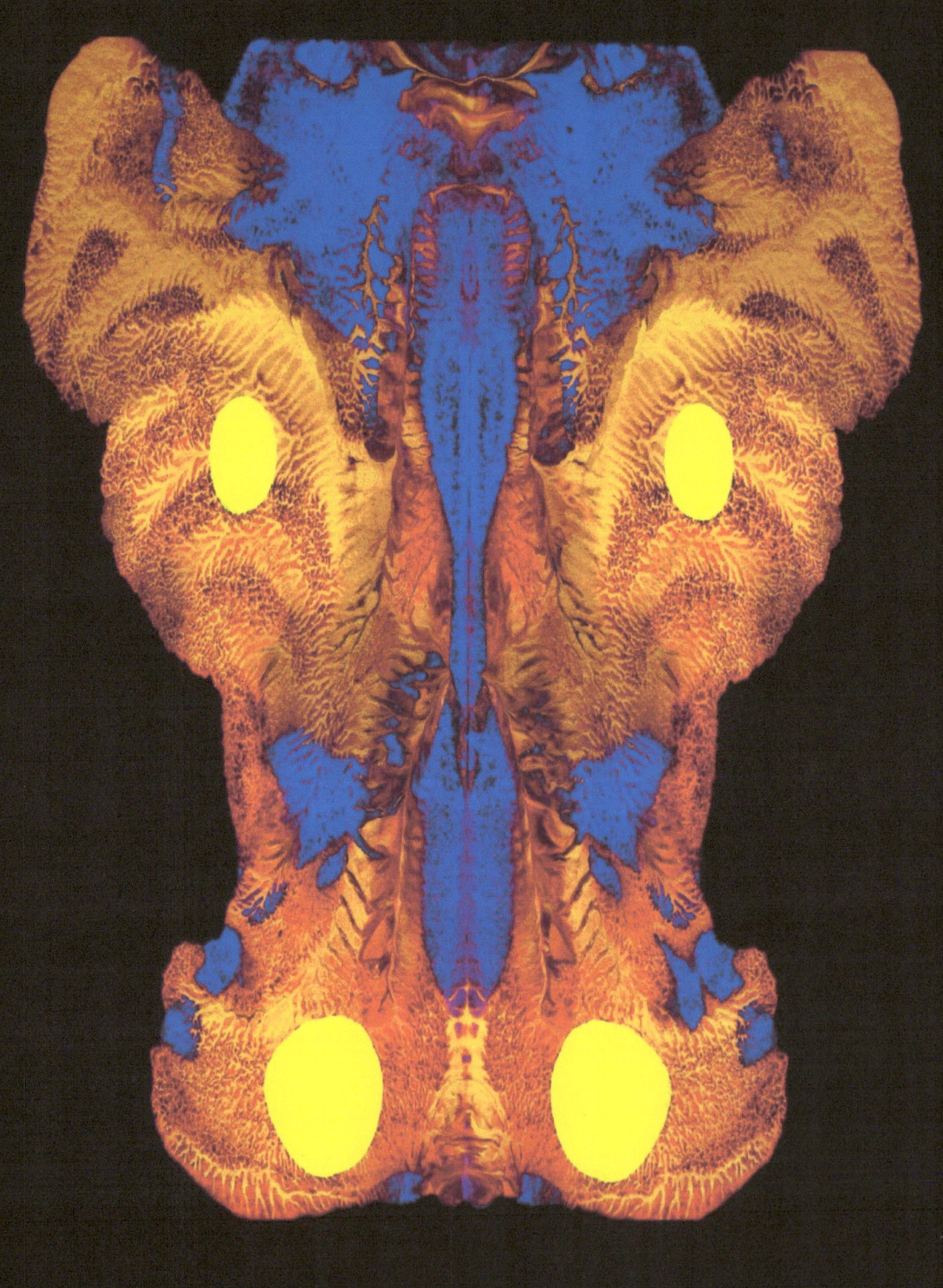

Image 164

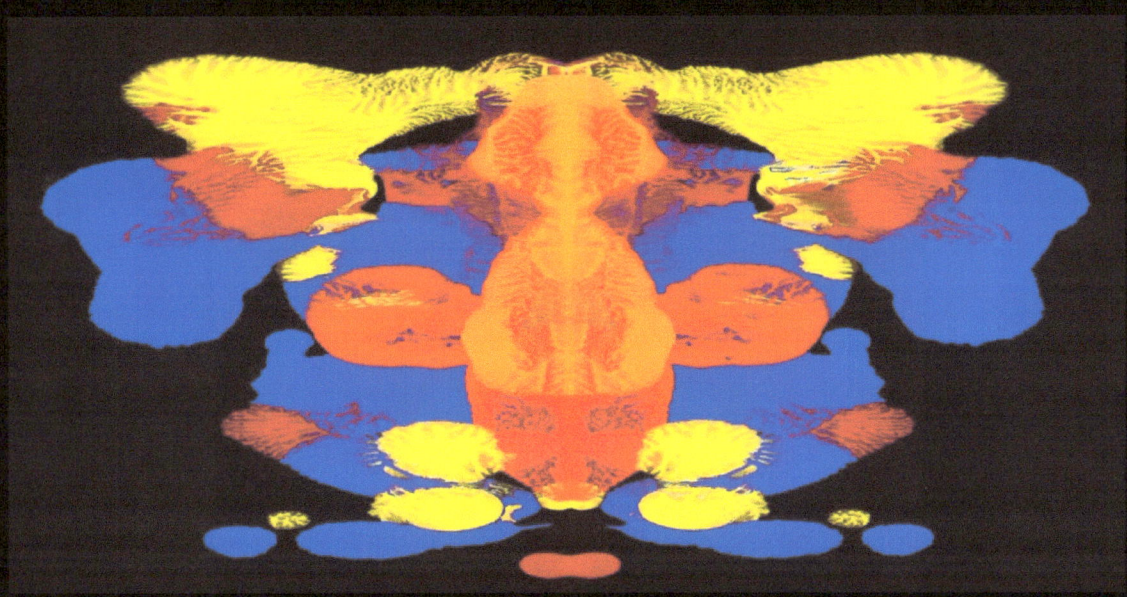

In Case You Were Wondering About the Process...

Fountain pens were still in common use when I started school. Like many kids, I probably learned how to create inkblot art by accident—spill some ink on a sheet of paper, fold it over, and voilà. Besides the anticipation of what might appear when I opened the paper, I liked the symmetry and ambiguity of the resulting images.

The same principle was used to make the art in this book, but instead of using bottled ink, most of the images were created with acrylic paint (and a few with dye). I prefer paint over ink because it is less runny and can result in interesting veining, and multiple colours can be applied simultaneously or added later.

To deal with the wrinkling and pronounced folds in the paper, I then create a digital scan which also permits for colour and size adjustments.

I'm not always sure which way to orient an image—interpretation is arbitrary—so if you have not already done so, turn the images upside down and look at them again. What do you see now? Remember, there are no right or wrong answers!

www.ingramcontent.com/pod-product-compliance
Lightning Source LLC
Chambersburg PA
CBHW051206220526
45473CB00003B/925